COOKING WITH ZAC

COOKING WITH ZAC

RECIPES FROM RUSTIC TO REFINED

ZAC POSEN

with Raquel Pelzel

RODALE.

RODALE wellness

Live happy. Be healthy. Get inspired.

Sign up today to get exclusive access to our authors, exclusive bonuses, and the most authoritative, useful, and cutting-edge information on health, wellness, fitness, and living your life to the fullest.

Visit us online at RodaleWellness.com
Join us at RodaleWellness.com/Join

Rodale books may be purchased for business or promotional use or for special sales. For information, please e-mail: BookMarketing@Rodale.com.

Printed in the United States of America

Rodale Inc. makes every effort to use acid-free ♾, recycled paper   .

Principal photography by Anna Williams
Food styling by Victoria Granof
Prop styling by Pamela Duncan Silver

Photographs on pages xiii, 2, 28–29, 62, 65, 67, 130, 133, 190, and 193 by Vanina Sorrenti and page xi by Stephen Posen

Book design by Rae Ann Spitzenberger

Library of Congress Cataloging-in-Publication Data is on file with the publisher.

ISBN 978–1–62336–776–3 hardcover
ISBN 978–1–63565–213–0 signed hardcover

Distributed to the trade by Macmillan

2 4 6 8 10 9 7 5 3 1 hardcover

Follow us @RodaleBooks on 🐦 📘 📌 📷

We inspire health, healing, happiness, and love in the world.
Starting with you.

To the many people who have encouraged
my love of food and cooking

CONTENTS

INTRODUCTION

I probably think about food just as much as I think about fashion. Ask anyone in my atelier and they'll tell you—I'm constantly bringing in homemade goodies to nourish my team. Food is a central component of my life, and my greatest joy comes from cooking up a delicious meal for friends, or going to my house in the country to cook all weekend long and then share the bounty.

For me, food and fashion are both sensory experiences, and the process is the same whether you're planning a meal or a fashion collection. I started designing clothes early on and presented my first runway collection when I was 21. During all of this time, cooking has provided me a respite, a special place to experiment creatively and take care of my closest friends and loved ones. Both disciplines count on careful planning, invention, technique, risk, presentation, and above all the desire to give pleasure—whether it's a VIP fitting or a friend coming over for dinner. Creating a menu is like designing the order of "looks" for a show, and ultimately, serving a meal is its own kind of performance.

In fashion and food, starting with the best-quality materials, be they silk or heirloom tomatoes, always makes the biggest difference. My commitment to fresh ingredients comes from my deep love of the natural world. To see a green pea developing on the vine and to know when to pick it at its most perfect moment is thrilling.

I have quite a wonderful garden on the grounds of my family's home in Bucks County, Pennsylvania. I find joy working in the garden, planting, planning, and watching the seedlings develop—it's really my form of meditation. We grow all kinds of organic produce and experiment with innovative methods of gardening and new, interesting crops. If we could grow mozzarella, we would! It's a family affair: My father, with my sister, Alexandra, and brother-in-law, Nils, turn the garden each spring, with weeding falling to my mother (who claims to love it). My little niece and nephew help with the picking (and nibbling), and of course I'm there planting and sowing and weeding and picking all along the way.

Like a good meal or a great piece of clothing, a vegetable garden takes thoughtful planning and lots of care. We learn from our mistakes and missteps and try to get it right the next time around. It's really a life practice and art. To me, gardening is part of the beauty of cooking in the same way that sourcing beautiful and inspiring fabric is part of the beauty of designing.

ZAC THE BAKER, ZAC THE MAKER, ZAC THE GROWER

As far back as I can remember, I wanted to be called Zachary "the Baker" Posen. To say that I've always been a bit obsessed with food is probably an understatement. Like many kids, I used to make play dough from scratch and turn it into "dinner" on my play stove. I'd roll plasticine cookies and bake elaborate "cakes." When I was a little older, perhaps 8 or 9, I remember moving on to real baking, like making linzer tart cookies with my Aunt Karen, for the holidays. Soon after, I dabbled in French pastry like croquembouche, turning cream puff shells and spun sugar into a gleaming pyramid of edible delight ensconced in a golden and ultra-delicate weave of sugar threads. Crafting layer cakes and centerpiece desserts is, in its own way, similar to making a gown. No wonder I became a fashion designer!

My culinary training, if you want to call it that, comes from my family's tradition of cooking together and sitting around a table full of people and food, everyone appreciating the art on their plate as much as the art on the walls of our loft. My dad always said, "The family who eats together stays together!" My mom, a corporate lawyer, always made sure to be home in time for dinner, to sit down and eat with the family. My dad, who is an artist and has his painting studio in our loft, became a fantastic cook, and he'd prepare most of our nightly meals.

My culinary education started early and knew no borders. It continued when I lived abroad to study fashion in London. I returned to New York from design school in London to launch my company, and since then I've had the opportunity to explore the world and continue my food education. My trips (some business, some pleasure) to Italy and France and throughout Europe for fashion shows, to Japan for collaborations, and to other far-flung corners of the globe from Mexico to the Caribbean have opened my eyes to rich cultures and wonderful foods and traditions—for example, the tender and puffy dumpling-esque "ravioli" of Sardinia and a wonderfully rich Bahamian curry (page 107).

A SEASONAL REPERTOIRE

This book is an eclectic mix that truly reflects the places from which I draw the most culinary inspiration: traditional Japanese dishes, handmade Italian dumplings, French-country fare, curry-spiced sautés and stews, Parisian-style scrambled eggs, flourless chocolate cake. The recipes follow the seasons—not just food and growing seasons, but also fashion seasons, because the two go hand in hand in my life. We begin with Spring and Summer, with fresh and bright recipes like raw corn salads, grilled spicy squid over greens, and a simple pasta twirled in a vibrant, herby pesto. Then we transition to Resort, a season featuring exotic fabrics and foods from faraway places like stone crab salad, linguini with clams, and an orange blossom Bundt cake. Next comes Fall and Winter, the times when I crave hearty foods like oxtail soup, pan-fried gnocchi, and pistachio carrot cake frosted with dulce de leche. The Holiday season, full of tradition, is probably my favorite because it's when people really come together to celebrate at the table with bold flavors and rich dishes like citrus spiced

duck, a prosciutto-wrapped beef tenderloin, creamed spinach, and chocolate croissant bread pudding so sweet and rich you need to clear out your afternoon for a nap!

My style of cooking and eating is all about balance. I can't imagine restricting myself to a regime of no cream or no butter or no carbohydrates. I love creamy sauces and decadent desserts, but I feel it's important to temper those excesses with healthy and clean foods like spiced lentils with quinoa, ramen soup, poached salmon, and sorbet made from nothing more than blended melon, a little mint, and a squeeze of honey. I also like to balance simple presentations with grand ones. So I'll make myself a very healthy kombu tea and then turn around and make a 24-layer crêpe and chestnut cream cake. It's like thinking about a collection that includes both chic and easy daywear as well as magnificent and intricate ball gowns.

Cooking does a lot of things for me: It's a place for creativity; it connects me to my family's traditions; it's nostalgic; it's about giving love and nurturing my loved ones. I am truly passionate about food and good ingredients and really enjoy cooking, eating, and entertaining. You'll find lots of ideas throughout the book for setting the ambience and creating good energy for receiving and entertaining guests. Cooking is about sharing—recipes, ideas, flavors, and stories. It can bring us closer to other cultures, build bridges, and create bonds and friendships. I hope your cooking adventures are rich and delicious and fill your kitchen and dining room with laughter, smiles, and great joy.

SPRING & SUMMER

After a long winter of braises and roasts, I am ready to lighten things up! I love the moment when the forsythia comes out with its gold Pantone color—forsythia is the harbinger of spring with those concentrated sparks of yellow on the branch that make me think of the tulips and lilacs that will be blooming within a few weeks. I'll venture out to forage for peppery-tender watercress that grows in the creek that runs through our farm in Pennsylvania. This is also when the wild leeks—also known as ramps—begin to break free of the earth and stand tall in their fragrant glory. Everything is coming out of dormancy and coming back to life! I'll celebrate the first cherry tomatoes twisted off the vine.

Gardening reminds me so much of fashion design—when you garden, you're always planning several seasons in advance. The vegetables I harvest in the height of summer and well into October arrive as seedlings in the very early spring (even late winter). It's just like fabrics arriving at the atelier in time for a new collection that will go down the runway months later. Both arrivals mark the beginning of a new season. This is the time to plot and plan and, above all, imagine.

Once early summer arrives, the garden begins to really show promise, offering tender greens and baskets full of herbs. In one fell swoop I transition from spring soups and softly flavored salads and pastas to big and bold summertime dishes like my dad's wonderfully citrusy-smoky slow-barbecued ribs and fresh-churned strawberry ice cream.

SPRING & SUMMER

SPRING WATERCRESS SOUP *Serves 4*

¾ pound asparagus, tough ends snapped off

1 medium leek, tough green tops and root end removed

1½ tablespoons extra-virgin olive oil

2 medium garlic cloves, roughly chopped

1 large white onion, finely chopped

1½ teaspoons fine sea salt, plus more to taste

1 large or 2 medium russet potatoes, peeled and chopped into ¼" cubes

1 piece (2" long) lemon peel (just the rind, not the white pith), finely chopped

3–4 cups store-bought or homemade vegetable or chicken broth (page 208)

¼ cup packed watercress

½ teaspoon freshly ground mixed peppercorns

¼ cup heavy cream (optional)

Crème fraîche (optional)

There is a magical moment in April when the most amazingly green and spicy watercress springs up in the creek running alongside our country house. I'm usually so excited to get outside after a long season indoors that I'll walk along the banks, picking cress to turn into a salad or this soup—it's so green and healthy that I'll eat it for lunch and skip the green juice! In this soup I add the cress right at the end, so it has just enough time to wilt slightly but doesn't sit long enough in the hot liquid to completely lose its vibrant chlorophyll-rich hue or dull its bite. The soup is lovely and delicate, and rich with vitamins. When cress isn't available, adding just about any tender greens will do, like spinach, escarole, or arugula—or even sweet early summer peas (this will make the soup slightly thicker).

1 Slice off the tops of the asparagus (keep the segment about 1" long) and set them aside for serving. Slice the remaining asparagus into 1" pieces. Slice the leek in half lengthwise and place it under cool running water to rinse the dirt and any sediment out from between the layers. Set the halves on a cutting board and slice them crosswise into 1" pieces.

2 Add 1 tablespoon of the olive oil and the garlic to a soup pot and then set the pot over medium heat. Once the garlic begins to sizzle, about 30 seconds, add the onion and leek. Cook, stirring often, until they just start to soften but don't brown, about 5 minutes. Stir in ¼ teaspoon of the salt and then stir in the potatoes and the lemon peel. Once the lemon is fragrant, after 1 minute or so, add 3 cups of the broth, increase the heat to high, and bring the soup to a boil.

3 Reduce the heat to medium-low and simmer gently, stirring occasionally, until the potatoes easily smash against the side of the pot, about 15 minutes. Increase the heat to medium-high, add the asparagus, and cover the pot. Cook until the asparagus is bright green and tender, 3 to 4 minutes. Turn off the heat, uncover, and add the watercress, 1 teaspoon of the salt, and the pepper. Stir to combine and taste, adjusting the salt and pepper as needed.

4 Blend the soup in batches (don't fill the blender more than two-thirds full with hot ingredients; otherwise, the steam builds up and you could end up with soup on your ceiling!) until there aren't any strings from the asparagus (you can even strain the soup through a fine-mesh sieve if you like). Return the blended soup to a clean pot. Add the cream, if using, and heat the soup until it is warmed through. Turn off the heat. If the consistency isn't thin enough for your taste, add the remaining 1 cup of broth.

5 Warm the remaining ½ tablespoon of olive oil in a small skillet over medium-high heat. Add the reserved asparagus tips and the remaining ¼ teaspoon of salt and cook, shaking the pan often, until the asparagus is tender, 3 to 6 minutes (depending on how thick the tips are). Divide the soup among bowls and serve each with a dollop of crème fraîche, if using, and sprinkled with a few asparagus tips.

Food/Fashion: Spring and Early Summer

From a fashion perspective, the Spring/Summer Collection leans to the feminine, to what's in bloom, and usually marks a return of a healthy glow—in fact, much like spring eating! Just like I eat more quick-cooked vegetables, salads, and "green" foods in the spring into summer, for my Spring/Summer Collection I look for softer textures and vibrancy in color. I want fabric to flow and be light and airy. I aim for a lightness of spirit.

CHILLED BORSCHT *Serves 4*

1½ teaspoons canola or grapeseed oil

¾ cup thinly sliced red cabbage

½ medium red onion, finely chopped

1¾ teaspoons fine sea salt

1½ pounds roasted beets, peeled and quartered

1½ tablespoons granulated sugar

Juice of ½ lemon

1 tablespoon champagne vinegar

3 cups store-bought or homemade chicken broth (page 208) or vegetable broth

½ cup crème fraîche

1 small cucumber, seeded and finely chopped

1 tablespoon finely chopped fresh dill

I have a confession to make: Often when I make borscht or order it at a restaurant, I'm only partly getting it because of its flavor. I love its intensely deep red color. Ladling the chilled soup into a bowl gives me the desire to dye every single one of my cotton shirts pink. While this isn't a family recipe, it most definitely is a dish I'm sure my ancestors, being Eastern European, enjoyed. I usually serve borscht cold, but it is really satisfying served warm, too.

1 Heat the canola or grapeseed oil in a small skillet over medium heat. Add the cabbage, onion, and ¼ teaspoon of the salt and cook, stirring often, until they are tender, 4 to 5 minutes. Turn off the heat and allow to cool slightly.

2 Combine the roasted beets, sugar, lemon juice, vinegar, the remaining 1½ teaspoons of salt, and the cooled cabbage-onion mixture in a blender. Add the broth and blend until velvety smooth. Taste and adjust with more salt if needed. Pour the soup into an airtight container and refrigerate until chilled, at least 2 hours.

3 Divide the borscht among bowls and top with a dollop of crème fraîche. Serve sprinkled with the chopped cucumber and dill.

Roasting Beets

Wrap each cleaned beet (trim the ends and scrub the beet well) in a square of aluminum foil so the beet is completely enclosed. Roast at 350°F for 1 to 1½ hours, depending on how large the beets are; you know they're done when a paring knife easily slips into the center without any resistance whatsoever. Cool the beets, then peel them. (Wear kitchen gloves if you don't want pink hands—and watch out for any surface, cutting board, or piece of clothing that might get stained by the beet juice!)

ARTICHOKES WITH DIJON–HERB AIOLI *Serves 4*

1 lemon, halved

4 large artichokes

1½ tablespoons Dijon mustard

1 teaspoon balsamic vinegar

2 tablespoons finely chopped fresh chives

1 tablespoon finely chopped fresh dill

2 teaspoons finely chopped fresh tarragon leaves

¼ teaspoon fine sea salt

¼ teaspoon freshly ground black pepper

1 cup extra-virgin olive oil

Artichokes are a must-have in my house. I love cooking them in boiling water until tender and then breaking off the leaves to dip into a homemade herby aioli (really just like mayonnaise minus the egg). Though simple, making aioli by hand requires some patience when adding the oil and exerting a little energy with a whisk. Set your prettiest bowl on the table for discarding artichoke leaves.

1 Squeeze the juice from one lemon half into a large bowl of cold water, and set the bowl aside. Trim the very end off of each artichoke stem, then use your fingers to break or snap off the tough outer leaves. Use kitchen shears to trim the leaves of the upper third of the artichoke, cutting them on a sharp 45° angle so you expose the tender leaves and create a cone shape toward the tip. Place the trimmed artichokes in the lemon water.

2 Fill a large pot half full with water and bring to a boil over high heat. Slice the remaining lemon half into quarters. Remove the artichokes from the lemon water and place them in the boiling water along with the quartered lemon. Set a smaller lid or a heat-safe plate on the artichokes to submerge them, and boil until a paring knife easily slips into the base of the biggest one, 25 to 30 minutes.

3 While the artichokes cook, make the aioli: Whisk together the mustard, vinegar, chives, dill, tarragon, salt, and pepper in a medium bowl. While whisking, add the olive oil in a very slow and steady drizzle. The mixture should become thick and creamy; if you add the oil too quickly, the aioli will break and look curdled. If this happens, whisk in 1 to 2 teaspoons of hot water to get back the creamy consistency.

4 Drain the artichokes and place them in a kitchen towel, squeezing a little to drain off any water. Divide the aioli into smaller bowls and serve with each artichoke.

Pickled Cucumber

1 English cucumber, very thinly sliced into rounds

3 tablespoons kosher salt

2 tablespoons apple cider vinegar

2 tablespoons mirin rice wine

1 tablespoon ponzu sauce

2 teaspoons honey

1 teaspoon toasted sesame oil

1 teaspoon granulated sugar

Salad

1 large fennel bulb, trimmed, halved, cored, and thinly sliced

1 lemon, ½ cut into wedges

2 bunches watercress, tough stems removed

Pinch of salt

10 large mint leaves, stacked, rolled, and sliced crosswise into thin ribbons

Crabs

1 large egg

Pinch plus ½ teaspoon sea salt

¾ cup panko bread crumbs

¾ cup corn flour

3–4 cups peanut or vegetable oil

4 cleaned soft-shell crabs

PAN-FRIED SOFT-SHELL CRAB OVER FENNEL SALAD WITH PICKLED CUCUMBER *Serves 4*

One of my favorite things is soft-shell crabs, which are really just crabs plucked out of the water while their shells are still soft from molting. I like to go on shopping adventures to Chinatown where I buy them already cleaned and ready to cook—they fry up quickly, and guests find them impressive. Here I toss them in a little corn flour and panko, then fry them until golden and crisp. A fresh and bright salad that highlights sharp and peppery watercress and thinly shaved fennel foils the crab's richness, while pickled cucumber offers a hint of sesame and sweetness. I make the cucumber pickle in the morning, so that when I get home, all I have to do is make the salad and pan-fry the crab. Once the cucumber is pickled, the rest comes together in 10 minutes (this is also great with the Cucumber-Turmeric Pickles on page 15).

1 *To make the pickled cucumber:* Place the cucumber slices in a medium bowl, add the salt, and toss to combine. (Yes, this seems like a lot of salt! It draws out the moisture in the cucumber and pickles it; don't worry, you'll wash all of it off before serving.) Set the cucumber aside at room temperature for at least 2 hours, or cover the bowl with plastic wrap and refrigerate for up to overnight.

2 Turn the cucumber slices out into a colander and rinse very well under cold running water. Rinse out the bowl, then return the cucumber to the bowl, and cover with very cold water. Use your hands to squeeze and grab the cucumber slices, massaging them in the water to pull out more salt. Drain the cucumber and return to a clean bowl. Whisk together the vinegar, rice wine, ponzu, honey, sesame oil, and sugar in a small bowl until the sugar is dissolved. Pour the seasoning over the cucumber, toss to combine, and refrigerate while you make the salad.

recipe continues

3 *To make the salad:* Add the fennel to a large bowl, squeeze in the lemon juice from half of the lemon, and toss together (the lemon juice helps to prevent browning). Add the watercress and a pinch of salt and gently toss with the fennel. Turn the mixture out onto a platter in an even layer and scatter the mint over the top.

4 *To make the crabs:* Whisk the egg with 2 tablespoons of water and a pinch of salt in a shallow dish (a pie plate works great) or bowl. Whisk the panko bread crumbs and corn flour together in a separate bowl. Heat ¼" of peanut or vegetable oil (3 to 4 cups) in a deep skillet over medium heat for 2 minutes.

5 Place the bread crumb mixture closest to the frying pan, the egg mixture in the middle, and the crabs farthest from the skillet. Take a crab, dip both sides in the egg wash, and then drag it through the bread crumb mixture so both sides are evenly coated. Carefully place the crab in the pan (be careful—take a step back after placing the crab in the pan because they sputter and spatter; I definitely do not wear my best outfit for frying crabs!). Repeat with the remaining crabs, cooking until they are golden brown on both sides, 7 to 8 minutes total. Transfer the crabs to a paper towel–lined cutting board, slice each one in half, and season with the remaining ½ teaspoon of salt while the crabs are hot.

6 Lay the crab halves on top of the salad. Place the cucumber slices on top and surround with lemon wedges for serving.

Soft-Shell Crab Sandwich
Take the fried soft-shell crabs and place on a toasted bun or roll. Top with the pickled cucumber. Add some mayonnaise (try making your own from the recipe on page 16) and a squeeze of Sriracha to the top bun half and serve.

CUCUMBER-TURMERIC PICKLES *Makes 1 pint*

¼ cup mirin rice wine

1 tablespoon distilled white vinegar

¼ cup granulated sugar

¼ cup fine sea salt

1 tablespoon freshly ground black pepper

3 sprigs fresh dill, stemmed and finely chopped

1½ tablespoons grated fresh turmeric or 2 teaspoons ground turmeric

4 Persian cucumbers or 1 English cucumber

Fresh turmeric is quickly becoming a staple in my refrigerator. I use it just like fresh ginger—scrape away the skin using the edge of a teaspoon, then finely chop or grate it into any dish. The flavor is earthy with a zesty, almost citrusy freshness—similar to comparing fresh ginger to dry ground ginger. In this pickle, the fresh turmeric tints the pickled cucumbers a beautiful shade of golden orange. If you can't find fresh turmeric, use half as much ground turmeric instead.

1 Whisk the rice wine, vinegar, sugar, salt, pepper, dill, and turmeric together in a medium bowl until the sugar and salt are both dissolved.

2 Use a mandoline or a chef's knife to slice the cucumbers into paper-thin disks. Add them to the mirin mixture—the cucumbers should be completely submerged (you can use a small plate to weight them down). Cover the bowl with plastic wrap and refrigerate for at least 6 hours or preferably overnight before serving.

2–MINUTE MAYO *Makes about 1 cup*

1 large egg yolk

1 tablespoon lemon juice or Meyer lemon juice

1 teaspoon Dijon mustard

½ teaspoon fine sea salt

½ cup canola oil

⅓ cup extra-virgin olive oil

Homemade mayonnaise tastes so good—it's infinitely better than anything you can buy, and you know what? It takes just 2 minutes to make. Of course, using it as a sandwich spread is a given—I also like to stir a generous spoonful into a sauce to give it a wonderfully glossy finish that adds a taste that's slightly tangier than butter or cream. You can add just about anything to mayo to season it to dress up a sandwich or to use as a dip, from Sriracha to crumbled blue cheese (thin with buttermilk for a dressing) or even a little grated garlic and lemon zest to accompany fried fish.

1 Add the egg yolk, lemon juice, mustard, salt, and 1 tablespoon of water to a blender and pulse to combine.

2 Add the canola oil and olive oil to a liquid measuring cup. With the blender running, incorporate the oil a few drips at a time, going very, very slowly (otherwise, the mayo could break). Once about ¼ cup of the oil is added and the mixture is thick, you can begin drizzling in the oil a little bit quicker, but still in a slow and steady stream—this should take about 1 minute.

3 Taste and adjust the seasoning with more salt if you like. Refrigerate the mayonnaise in an airtight container for up to 5 days (not that it will last that long since it's so tasty!).

WEEKENDS AT
THE POTTING SHED

When I was a child, my family would often drive up to the Berkshires in Massachusetts for weekend visits with my god-mother, Nancy, a brilliant calligrapher/designer. Nancy lived in a wonderful home called the Potting Shed that had been part of the historic Wheatleigh estate near Tanglewood. It is a magical place, with an intensely special juju—maybe leftover good vibes from having been a renowned concert venue back in the day (Jimi Hendrix even played there!). Nancy's home had a glass roof that magically brought the outside in. I slept on a futon under the sloping glass ceiling surrounded by plants and looking up at stars or at the pattern of the rain. Nancy had an incredible ability to welcome others into her magical home. It was here that I was introduced to the art of casual entertaining and large, interesting parties.

"I still love the look and whimsy of edible flowers."

In the morning I'd walk outside and be greeted by a myriad of clownlike-faced pansies in every color of the rainbow. Besides enjoying the flowers, I could pick and even eat them! I still love the look and whimsy of edible flowers. It was also at the Potting Shed where I learned how to create beautiful and rustic flower arrangements out of wild fiddlehead ferns and lilies of the valley that I gathered on the grounds. Here I fell in love with nature, gardening, and the seemingly effortless style of country entertaining. Nancy had this calm naturalness about her; she could prepare the most elaborate meal while still engaging guests. I actually think that one of her tricks was delegating small tasks to me! Helping her out made me feel proprietary and like my efforts contributed to the overall success of the party.

ASPARAGUS WITH EDIBLE FLOWERS *Serves 4*

2 teaspoons plus ¼ teaspoon fine sea salt

1 pound asparagus (any kind—pencil thin or finger thick), ends snapped off

1 tablespoon sherry vinegar

1 teaspoon finely chopped shallot

1 teaspoon Dijon mustard

¼ teaspoon finely ground black pepper

3 tablespoons extra-virgin olive oil

12 edible flowers, stacked and very thinly sliced into ribbons (see page 20)

There is a certain amount of Victoriana to this dish—the long and lanky spears of interlinking asparagus remind me of calligraphy, and the edible flowers highlight and lend a note of genteel elegance that I find so appealing. It's the edible flower bits, thinly sliced like confetti, that augment the dish's beauty. Even though this side dish looks so stunning, it couldn't be more simple—it's really just plunging the asparagus in boiling water for a few minutes, then shocking it in ice water before drizzling a classic vinaigrette over the top. Simple, fast, elegant, healthy, perfect!

1 Fill a large bowl with ice and water and set aside. Fill a large and deep skillet (preferably one with straight sides) with 1" of water. Add 2 teaspoons of the salt and bring to a boil over high heat.

2 Reduce the heat to medium and add the asparagus spears. Blanch until the spears are tender but still have snap, 2 to 4 minutes, depending on how thin or thick the asparagus are (pencil-thin asparagus will finish quickly, while thick asparagus will take longer to cook).

3 Drain the asparagus in a colander and plunge into the ice water to stop the cooking. Once they are cool to the touch, pat them dry and transfer the asparagus to a paper towel–lined plate.

4 Whisk together the vinegar, shallot, mustard, remaining ¼ teaspoon of salt, and the pepper in a small bowl. Slowly whisk in the olive oil until the vinaigrette is creamy and emulsified.

5 Place the asparagus on a platter. Drizzle with the vinaigrette and sprinkle the edible flowers over the top.

USING EDIBLE FLOWERS

Treating myself to weekly bouquets of seasonal blooms is like bringing instant joy and peacefulness into any space. Flowers are an enormous source of inspiration for me—in the atelier, I use their shape, color, and structure to dream up gowns and corseting and fabrics. At home, I make sure a flowering orchid or a colorful arrangement of blooms is a constant in the living room. When I'm out in the country, there's always a vase on the table holding stems just clipped from the garden to bring the outside in. And in my cooking, I just love the color, whimsy, and spirit that edible flowers bring to a dish. There are lots to choose from—just be sure that yours are chemical- and pesticide-free, and preferably grown according to organic standards. Here's a list of my favorites—unless otherwise noted, you can use the whole blossom. Whole petals are romantic; a chiffonade is extra colorful; and small whole flowers are so incredibly evocative.

- Begonia petals
- Herb blossoms (chive, lavender, and thyme; chopped or whole)
- Hibiscus
- Impatiens
- Marigold (calendula) petals
- Nasturtium leaves (so nice and spicy!)
- Pansies
- Rose petals
- Scented geranium
- Violets
- Zucchini squash blossoms (chiffonade into fine ribbons)

FIRST TOMATOES SAUCE *Serves 4*

1 tablespoon plus
1 teaspoon kosher salt

1 pound pasta (Any
shape works, so use
your favorite!)

4 medium garlic
cloves, roughly
chopped

½ medium yellow
onion, finely chopped

¼ cup extra-virgin
olive oil

4 cups (2 pints) small
cherry or grape
tomatoes (halved if
they're on the big side)

1 cup dry white wine

¼ teaspoon freshly
ground black pepper

1 teaspoon honey

3 tablespoons fresh
chèvre, 2 tablespoons
heavy cream, or
1 tablespoon unsalted
butter

½ cup thinly sliced
fresh basil leaves

Cherry tomatoes are the first to ripen in the garden, and all spring I look forward to turning them into a wonderfully quick pasta sauce. For every tomato I pick, I pop one in my mouth. It doesn't take much to coax out these flavors for a fresh and bright sauce for pasta. Start the sauce while the water comes to a boil. The sauce will be finished by the time the pasta is at the al dente stage.

1 Bring a large pot of water to a boil over high heat with 1 tablespoon of the salt. Add the pasta and cook until it is just a little shy of being al dente—when you bite into a piece, you think it still needs a minute or two. Ladle ½ cup of the cooking water into a heat-safe mug or cup and drain the pasta.

2 While the water comes to a boil, make the sauce: Add the garlic, onion, and olive oil to a large skillet (don't turn on the heat yet). Turn the heat on to medium and cook, stirring occasionally, until the onion begins to soften, about 5 minutes. Stir in the remaining 1 teaspoon of salt and then add the tomatoes and increase the heat to medium-high. Cook, stirring occasionally, until the tomato skin starts to rip and the tomatoes begin to burst and get juicy, about 12 minutes.

3 Increase the heat to high and add the wine and pepper. Give the sauce a stir, let the wine come up to a hard simmer, then reduce the heat to medium-low and cover the pan. Cook until the tomatoes deflate, 2 to 3 minutes, then uncover the pan, stir in the honey, and let the juices reduce by half, about 2 minutes.

4 Add the pasta and the reserved pasta cooking water to the pan and continue to cook, stirring very often—you want to keep the pasta moving, and you can also give the pan a good jerky shake every now and then—until the pasta is perfectly al dente, 1 to 2 minutes longer.

5 Stir in whatever finishing accent you are adding: either chèvre, cream, or butter. Stir in the basil, saving some to sprinkle over the top, and serve immediately.

FLATBREAD OF SWEET EXCESS *Serves 4*

½ cup red or Marsala wine

3 tablespoons honey (if using Marsala, use only 2 tablespoons)

6 pitted, dried prunes, quartered

Flour, for rolling

1 ball (8 ounces) store-bought or homemade pizza dough

Cornmeal, for transferring the pizza to the oven

3 ounces chèvre (fresh goat's milk cheese)

2 tablespoons extra-virgin olive oil

¼ teaspoon red-pepper flakes

Flaky sea salt

2 tablespoons truffle butter

8 medium basil leaves, stacked, rolled lengthwise, and sliced crosswise into thin ribbons

Sweet, rich, and savory, this super crisp flatbread is wonderful cut into small squares and served as an hors d'oeuvre or even after dinner with a cheese course (substitute a drizzle of honey for the red-pepper flakes). Instead of basil, you can also try it draped with prosciutto after baking and finished with a chiffonade of arugula leaves.

1 Place a pizza stone on the middle oven rack and preheat the oven to 475°F. (If you don't have a pizza stone, you can use a rimmed baking sheet.)

2 Bring the wine and honey to a simmer in a small saucepan over medium heat, stirring occasionally. Add the prunes and continue to cook, stirring occasionally, until only 2 to 3 tablespoons of liquid remains, about 10 minutes. Turn off the heat and set aside for 15 minutes.

3 Lightly flour your work surface and place the pizza dough on top. Lightly flour the top of the dough, then roll it into a thin circle, about ⅛" thick, giving the dough a quarter turn every stroke or two to keep it from sticking and adding more flour beneath the dough whenever it starts to stick.

4 Heavily sprinkle a pizza peel with cornmeal and transfer the dough to the peel. (If you don't have a pizza peel, a large sheet of parchment paper works, too; set it on a rimless sheet pan—or an upside-down rimmed sheet pan—sprinkle it with cornmeal, and then place the dough on top and slide the piece of parchment right onto the pizza stone.) Dollop the dough with the goat cheese. Sprinkle with the drained prunes and then drizzle with olive oil. Sprinkle with the red-pepper flakes and salt to taste, then bake until the crust is crisp and browned, 8 to 10 minutes.

5 Remove the pizza from the oven and quickly scatter little bits of the truffle butter all over the surface. Sprinkle with the basil, slice, and serve.

CLASSIC MARGHERITA PIZZA *Serves 4*

Flour, for rolling

1 ball (8 ounces) store-bought or homemade pizza dough

Cornmeal, for transferring the pizza to the oven

¼–½ cup store-bought tomato sauce, Lemon Zest Pomodoro (page 145), or First Tomatoes Sauce (page 21)

¼ pound fresh mozzarella, sliced into thin rounds

2 tablespoons extra-virgin olive oil

Flaky sea salt

¼ cup finely grated Parmigiano-Reggiano cheese

10 basil leaves, stacked, rolled lengthwise, and sliced crosswise into thin ribbons

The trick to a great pizza is to keep toppings light—and by light, I don't mean low-calorie, I mean spare in amount so the crust doesn't sog out. It's so disappointing to pick up a slice of pizza and have the entire tip of the triangle sag under the weight of the toppings! When adding the sauce to the dough, add it to the middle and then use the back of a large spoon or ladle to spread it out in gradually increasing circles.

1   Place a pizza stone on the middle oven rack and preheat the oven to 475°F. (If you don't have a pizza stone, you can use a rimmed baking sheet.)

2   Lightly flour your work surface and place the pizza dough on top. Lightly flour the top of the dough, then roll it into a thin circle, about ⅛" thick, giving the dough a quarter turn every stroke or two (this will help keep it from sticking) and adding more flour beneath the dough whenever it starts to stick.

3   Heavily sprinkle a pizza peel with cornmeal and transfer the dough to the peel. (If you don't have a pizza peel, a large sheet of parchment paper works, too; set it on a rimless sheet pan— or an upside-down rimmed sheet pan—sprinkle it with corn-meal, and then place the dough on top and slide the piece of parchment right onto the pizza stone.) Add ¼ cup of marinara sauce to the center of the dough (or more if you like a saucier pizza) and use a ladle or the backside of a large spoon to spread it out in large swooping circles. Place the mozzarella on top of the marinara, and then drizzle with the olive oil. Sprinkle with the salt to taste and then with the Parmigiano-Reggiano. Slide the pizza onto the stone and bake until the crust is crisp and browned, 8 to 10 minutes.

4   Remove from the oven and place the pizza on a large platter. Sprinkle with the basil, slice, and serve.

MY LOVE AFFAIR WITH PIZZA

As a born and bred New Yorker, I probably ate a slice of pizza every day from the time I had teeth to the time I graduated high school! My most beloved pizza place no longer exists; it was called the Pizza Box on Bleecker Street. I would go there every day for a slice and hang out in the garden out back. They made a really good, thin pizza with a nice, crisp crust and a good sauce-to-cheese ratio.

When I went to university in London, the owners of a small restaurant called Ciao Bella on Lamb's Conduit took a shine to me and essentially kept me alive with their wonderful cooking. They fed me their arugula and prosciutto pizza and fortified me with an espresso every morning. They watched over me and, when I was short on funds, even lent me a few hundred pounds to buy fabric and just generally survive in pricey London.

"Pizza is always a sure bet."

I began experimenting with pizza at the farm in Pennsylvania because I knew that, with family and cousins, nieces, and nephews of all ages coming to visit, pizza is always a sure bet. I began making my own pizza dough and creating all kinds of fun and bespoke toppings like prunes with goat cheese and truffle butter (page 22) or pizzas strewn with honey and edible flowers. It's one of my favorite ways to greet guests when they come to our home in Bucks County—with a welcoming and piping hot slice!

GARDEN QUICHE

Makes one 9½" quiche

1 large golden beet, ends trimmed and beet peeled

A drizzle plus 1 tablespoon extra-virgin olive oil

A pinch plus 1 teaspoon fine sea salt

Pie dough for 1 crust (½ recipe My Favorite Pie Dough, page 50, or store-bought is fine, too)

All-purpose flour, for rolling

1 medium leek, white and light green parts only, finely chopped

½ teaspoon freshly ground black pepper

6 cups chopped Swiss chard leaves

4 large eggs

⅔ cup whole milk

½ cup heavy cream

1 teaspoon curry powder (or turmeric for a milder flavor)

1 cup grated Gruyère cheese

2 ounces chèvre (fresh goat's milk cheese), crumbled

1 tablespoon finely chopped fresh dill, chives, or tarragon

10 basil leaves, stacked, rolled lengthwise, and sliced crosswise into thin ribbons

Quiche is one of the best dishes to make when entertaining because it can be made ahead and served at room temperature and is great for breakfast, brunch, lunch, or an early evening dinner. This is my favorite kind of quiche—a bit of a garden hodgepodge. Like pasta, quiche is amenable to variations, so check out the next page for some ideas. Curry adds a little color and a hint of warmth to the quiche—for a more mellow taste, you can substitute turmeric.

1 Adjust an oven rack to the lower-middle position and preheat the oven to 375°F. Set the beet in the middle of a large square of aluminum foil and drizzle with olive oil and a pinch of salt. Tightly enclose the beet in the foil and roast it until a paring knife easily slips into the center, 1 hour to 1 hour and 15 minutes.

2 Meanwhile, set the pie dough on a lightly floured surface and sprinkle the top of the dough with more flour. Roll the pie dough to between a ⅛" to ¼" thickness, moving the round often and re-flouring the top and beneath the dough to ensure the dough doesn't stick. Transfer the pie crust to a 9½" pie plate, fitting it into the edges and sides and crimping the edges. Use a fork to prick the dough all over, then place the pie plate in the refrigerator to chill for 20 minutes.

3 Line the pie crust with parchment paper or aluminum foil, and add enough pie weights or dry beans to cover the bottom. Bake it for 15 minutes. At this point the beet should be about done—test it and if it is tender, remove it from the oven and set aside to cool. Carefully remove the parchment or foil from the pie plate (if using dry beans, discard them; if using pie weights, set them aside to cool) and return it to the oven until the bottom of the crust isn't shiny and the crust just starts to color, 5 to 8 minutes. Remove the crust from the oven. Reduce the oven temperature to 350°F.

4 While the pie crust bakes, prepare the quiche filling: Heat the remaining 1 tablespoon of oil in a large skillet over medium heat. Add the leek, ½ teaspoon of the salt, and ¼ teaspoon of the pepper and cook, stirring often, until the leek is soft and shiny but not browned, 3 to 4 minutes. Add the chard and cook, stirring often, until it wilts, about 1 minute. Turn off the heat, transfer the mixture to a medium bowl, and set it aside to cool for 10 to 15 minutes, then spread it over the bottom of the pie crust. Once the beet is cool enough to handle, peel and chop it into bite-size chunks, then sprinkle it over the leek mixture.

5 Whisk the eggs, milk, cream, remaining ½ teaspoon salt, remaining ¼ teaspoon pepper, and the curry (or turmeric) together in a large bowl. Add the Gruyère and goat cheese and stir to combine, then stir in the dill (or other herb) and basil. Pour the filling over the vegetables in the pie crust. Return the quiche to the oven and bake until the filling is puffed and golden, 50 minutes to 1 hour.

6 Remove the quiche from the oven and set aside to cool for at least 1 hour before slicing and serving. The quiche can be served warm or at room temperature.

Love and Quiches

When making quiche, please—oh—please don't feel that you need to stick to the recipe. Quiche is like a blank canvas that happily takes on a host of flavors and seasonings.

If you don't have . . .	*Try*
Golden beet	Potato, sweet potato, rutabaga
Leek	Scallions, shallot, red or sweet onion
Swiss chard	Beet tops, spinach
Heavy cream	Coconut milk, whole milk
Curry powder	Turmeric, garam masala, ras el hanout
Gruyère	Mild cheddar, gouda, havarti
Goat's milk cheese	Blue cheese, feta, ricotta
Dill	Basil, cilantro, fennel tops, mint, parsley
Basil	Any one of the following: cilantro, mint, parsley, tarragon, thyme

CRISPY TEMPURA VEGETABLES *Serves 4*

Vegetables

4–6 cups grapeseed or canola oil, for frying

½ cup potato starch

⅓ cup plus 1 tablespoon all-purpose flour

½ teaspoon fine sea salt

1 cup seltzer or club soda

¾ pound vegetables such as asparagus with tough ends snapped off, slender carrots, topped and tailed green beans, trimmed scallions, okra, sliced lotus root, thin eggplant slices, or slices or planks of sweet potato

Dipping Sauce

¼ cup shoyu (Japanese soy sauce)

2 tablespoons mirin rice wine

1 tablespoon dry sake

1 tablespoon lime juice

½ teaspoon freshly grated gingerroot

¼ teaspoon toasted sesame oil

1 scallion, very thinly sliced

In Kyoto, there are a few secret restaurants that specialize in *only* tempura. The lightness of their batter and creativity in the nibbles being fried create a real delicacy that is never boring, greasy, or heavy. The batter on tempura vegetables should be thin, crispy, and delicate, like the thin crystallized surface of frost that clings to blades of grass in the early spring (can you tell I am super picky about my tempura?). The trick is to combine potato starch with seltzer water. The flour should just be like a dusting on the vegetable, not a thick, doughy coating. If you're a fan of crunchy tempura, you can roll the battered vegetables in a little panko bread crumbs before frying. And if you have a splatter screen to place over the pan, now's the time to break it out—it definitely comes in handy to prevent oil splashing onto your hands or forearms when the vegetables fry.

1 Pour enough oil into a medium skillet (the vegetables should fit comfortably in the pan) to fill it 1" deep. Heat the oil over high heat until an instant-read thermometer registers 360°F.

2 *To make the dipping sauce:* While the oil heats, whisk together the shoyu, mirin, sake, lime juice, ginger, sesame oil, and scallion in a medium bowl. Divide among four small dipping bowls and set aside.

3 *To make the vegetables:* Whisk the potato starch, flour, and salt together in a medium bowl. Then whisk in the seltzer.

4 Dunk a piece of a vegetable in the batter and add it to the oil—it should immediately be surrounded by tiny bubbles and begin frying. If it doesn't, continue to heat the oil until it does. Batter the remaining pieces and add them to the oil, taking care not to crowd the pan. Use a frying spider, chopsticks, or a fork to turn the vegetables often as they cook. Fry until they are crisp and golden, 1½ to 2 minutes.

4 Transfer the vegetables to a wire rack to drain and cool slightly before serving with the dipping sauce.

SWEET PEA RAVIOLI WITH SAGE BROWNED BUTTER

Serves 8 or 4 with leftovers (makes 40 large ravioli)

Pasta Dough

3 cups all-purpose flour, plus extra for rolling

1 teaspoon fine sea salt, plus 1 tablespoon for the pasta water

2 large eggs, lightly beaten

2 tablespoons extra-virgin olive oil

Ravioli Filling

3 cups fresh peas (or frozen petit peas)

6 ounces (about ⅔ cup) chèvre (fresh goat's milk cheese)

½ cup ricotta cheese

½ cup finely grated Parmigiano-Reggiano cheese

1½ teaspoons plus a pinch of fine sea salt

½ teaspoon finely grated lemon zest

1 cup finely chopped roasted and salted shelled pistachios

¼ cup finely chopped fresh basil leaves

2 large eggs, lightly beaten

Browned Butter

6 tablespoons unsalted butter

24 fresh sage leaves

Pinch of coarse sea salt

Our hands are really our best tools—for cooking, creating, sewing. Everything! I work with my hands all day draping, cutting, and drawing. But I still love to come home and knead pasta dough by hand. Making dough by hand brings a whole extra level of love to the dish, not to mention it's great exercise! That said, you can, of course, make the dough in a stand mixer using a dough hook if you want a more hands-off experience. Just follow the visual clues below for mixing. Filled with a sweet pea and pistachio filling and finished with sage browned butter, these ravioli sing of spring. You can freeze uncooked ravioli flat on a sheet pan and then transfer them to a freezer-safe resealable plastic bag for up to 3 months. Pop them in boiling water, and a restaurant-worthy dinner is minutes away!

1 *To make the pasta dough:* Whisk the flour and 1 teaspoon of the salt together in a medium bowl. Make a well in the center and add the eggs and olive oil. Use a fork to slowly incorporate the eggs and oil into the flour mixture. Once the eggs and oil are incorporated and the mixture looks pretty crumbly and dry, drizzle in ¼ cup of water. Get your fingers in the dough and start squeezing, pressing, and rubbing the dough together, kneading it in the bowl until the dough is very silky and smooth. This will take 8 to 10 minutes—it will take at least 3 or 4 minutes for the dough ball to come together. Cover the dough ball with a damp towel and set aside for at least 30 minutes and up to 1 hour to rest.

2 *To make the ravioli filling:* If using fresh peas, blanch them in boiling water until they are tender and no longer starchy, 1 to 2 minutes. Plunge the blanched peas into an ice water bath to stop the cooking, then drain in a fine-mesh sieve and transfer them to a blender. If using frozen peas, rinse them under warm

recipe continues

*Making homemade
pasta dough for ravioli
takes an investment of
time—it isn't exactly the
kind of thing most people
cook on a weekday night
(unless you're a little
crazy like me!). When
I'm hosting a dinner and
making a more labor-in-
tensive dish like this,
I'll bundle the dish with
a simple starter, like a
puréed soup or simple
garden salad (perhaps
with a bright and fun
miso-yuzu vinaigrette
like the one on page
144), and an easy
dessert—like a simple
berry tart made with
store-bought dough.*

water in a sieve, shake off the liquid, and add them to a blender. Add the goat cheese, ricotta, Parmigiano-Reggiano, 1½ teaspoons of the salt, the lemon zest, and all but 2 tablespoons of the pistachios. Blend until rough textured. Transfer the mixture to a medium bowl and stir in the basil. Transfer the mixture to a piping bag fitted with a large round tip or to a resealable plastic bag with one corner cut away for easy piping, then refrigerate the filling (the filling can be made a few hours in advance).

3 Divide the dough into eight equal pieces and sprinkle the top and bottom of each with flour. Set six dough balls aside. Sprinkle your work surface with flour. Set up your pasta machine according to the manufacturer's instructions and begin to run the pasta through the machine's largest setting. Flour the top and bottom of the dough again and run it through the largest setting a second time. Repeat with each setting until you get to the second to thinnest setting (you may need to halve the strip of pasta if it gets too long to handle easily).

4 Place the pasta on the floured work surface. Starting 2" away from one side, squeeze the pastry bag to roughly dollop about 1 tablespoon of filling in the center of the dough. Move 2" down and repeat. Repeat as many times as possible, leaving a 2" border at the end. Add 1 tablespoon of water and a pinch of salt to the beaten eggs and use a fork to combine. Use a pastry brush to paint a square around each dollop of pasta filling (when you lay the second sheet of pasta on top, the egg wash acts like glue to seal the edges together).

5 Run a second ball of pasta through the machine and lay it over the first sheet. Press down along the top and bottom edges and then between each mound of filling to seal it in. Use a knife or a decorative pasta wheel to divide the long sheet into individual squares. Set the ravioli on a flour-dusted baking sheet and cover with a damp towel. Repeat with the remaining dough and the remaining filling.

6 *To make the browned butter sauce:* Add the butter to a small skillet and melt over medium heat. Reduce the heat to medium-low, add the sage leaves and a pinch of salt, and cook, swirling the butter in the pan often, until the butter is nutty brown and fragrant, 4 to 6 minutes. Turn off the heat and drizzle a little onto a large platter; set the rest aside.

7 Bring a large pot of water to a boil (or bring two pots of water to a boil to cook two batches at once). Add the remaining 1 tablespoon salt and about six of the ravioli to the pot (try not to overcrowd the pot; otherwise, the pasta could stick together) and cook until they rise to the surface, 1 to 2 minutes. Use a slotted spoon to transfer the ravioli to the buttered platter. Repeat with the remaining ravioli, and drizzle the remaining butter and sage over the top. Sprinkle the remaining pistachios over the pasta and serve.

RISOTTO CON FUNGHI

Serves 4

1 cup dried mushrooms (preferably porcinis)

4 tablespoons unsalted butter

1 medium yellow onion, finely chopped

1 teaspoon fine sea salt

1⅓ cups Arborio rice

3 tablespoons dry vermouth

3 cups warmed store-bought or homemade chicken broth (page 208)

1 tablespoon extra-virgin olive oil

3 peeled garlic cloves, smashed

1 pound morels, soaked to remove dirt, and halved if large

1 cup finely grated Parmigiano-Reggiano cheese

My mom has been making risotto forever. She always makes it in a blue enamel-coated cast-iron pot that she received as a wedding gift 50 years ago. She tells me the recipe came from Craig Claiborne's *New York Times Cookbook*, which was the classic go-to cookbook when she was learning her way around the kitchen. Essential to good risotto is using the right rice, Arborio, and paying constant attention to it for the 20 minutes it takes to cook. And the trick to great risotto con funghi is using dried porcini mushrooms. Soak them in hot water for at least 20 minutes (you can do this in advance: the longer, the better), then use the liquid from the mushrooms as part of the first liquid you add to the rice. This way, the rice absorbs the intense flavor of the mushrooms. You can always add bits of cooked asparagus or peas at the end, though I am a purist with respect to risotto and like it best the way my mom makes it: with love. And just mushrooms.

1 Place the dried mushrooms in a bowl and add enough hot water to submerge them. Cover the bowl with plastic wrap and soak for 20 minutes. Set a fine-mesh sieve over a bowl and strain the mushrooms (save the soaking liquid), then finely chop them and set aside. Pour the mushroom soaking liquid into a measuring cup—you want 1 cup; discard the rest (or freeze it for veggie stock).

2 Melt 2 tablespoons of the butter in a medium pot (preferably enameled cast iron) over medium heat. Add the onion and ½ teaspoon of the salt and cook, stirring often, until the onion is golden and just starting to brown around the edges, about 5 minutes.

3 Add the rice and stir it in, continuing to stir the rice every 30 seconds or so until it turns completely opaque white, 2 to 3 minutes. Add the vermouth and let it warm and bubble just long enough to burn off the alcohol, 2 to 3 minutes. Add the mushroom soaking liquid, increase the heat to medium-high,

and cook, stirring occasionally, until three-quarters of the liquid is absorbed, 4 to 5 minutes. You don't need to stir the risotto constantly—just enough so the rice doesn't stick to the bottom of the pan and the liquid doesn't settle on top of the rice.

4 Once the liquid is three-quarters absorbed, add 1 cup of broth. Repeat, stirring occasionally, until the broth is mostly absorbed (it should still pool a little at the bottom of the pot). Add another cup of broth and continue to cook the rice, stirring occasionally (now you have added 3 cups of liquid) until the broth is three-quarters absorbed. (The rice shouldn't take more than 20 minutes total to cook.)

5 While the risotto cooks, make the morels: Melt 1 tablespoon of the butter in a large skillet over medium heat. Add the olive oil and garlic. Once the garlic becomes fragrant, after about 2 minutes, increase the heat to medium-high and add the morels along with the remaining ½ teaspoon of salt. Cook, stirring often, until the morels are tender, 4 to 5 minutes. Turn off the heat and set the morels aside.

6 Add the last cup of broth to the risotto (all 4 cups of liquid—broth and mushroom soaking water—have now been added). Let it absorb by half instead of three-quarters (this should be at just about the 20-minute mark). Stir in the remaining 1 tablespoon of butter, followed by the grated cheese and the chopped mushrooms. Turn off the heat. The risotto should be very creamy and almost soupy looking. The rice will continue to expand between the time you finish cooking and when you start eating. Divide the risotto among four bowls and serve topped with the morels.

HERBED CROWN ROAST OF LAMB
Serves 4 (with a few lamb rib chops left over)

2 racks of lamb (8 ribs each), frenched and formed into a crown roast

3 teaspoons kosher salt

1 teaspoon freshly ground black pepper

8 medium garlic cloves, minced

1 tablespoon extra-virgin olive oil

1½ tablespoons Dijon mustard

1 tablespoon finely chopped fresh mint leaves

2 teaspoons finely chopped fresh rosemary

1 teaspoon curry powder

1 teaspoon dried onion powder

¼ teaspoon ground cinnamon

A crown roast of lamb is my idea of celebration. It's such a table stunner—positively regal sitting there with the leggy bones arching up from the meat. For an especially stunning presentation, ask your butcher to "french" the bones (meaning to scrape the meat off of the top of the bones) then cover them with foil or little paper frills (little decorative caps that cover the end of the bone) before roasting. I figure on three chops per person—this is a generous main dish serving. The curry powder adds more color and warmth than it does an Indian flavor because the mustard and herbs are the tastes that truly dominate. You can substitute turmeric if you like, or leave it out entirely. Simple boiled potatoes rolled around in melted butter and finished with chopped parsley are a perfect accessory.

1 Preheat the oven to 425°F. Line a roasting pan with aluminum foil and place the crown roast on top. Season the outside and inside of the roast with 1 teaspoon of the salt and the pepper. If you want to prevent the tips of the rib bones from turning dark, cover each tip individually with aluminum foil or paper frills.

2 Stir together the garlic, olive oil, mustard, mint, rosemary, curry powder, onion powder, cinnamon, and the remaining 2 teaspoons of salt in a small bowl. Rub the paste over the outside and inside of the roast.

3 Cook the lamb until an instant-read thermometer inserted into the meatiest part of the roast reads 130° to 135°F for medium-rare, about 35 to 40 minutes. Remove the roast from the oven, transfer to a serving platter, and loosely tent with foil. Let the lamb rest for 10 minutes before carving and serving.

FOUR STEPS TO PAN SAUCE

A pan sauce can elevate a steak, pan-seared chicken breast, or even a celebratory roast like the Herbed Crown Roast of Lamb (page 37) into a more cohesive and "finished" dish. Good thing that making a pan sauce is so simple—follow these steps and try it out!

1. If you didn't cook the meat or fish in a skillet, transfer any pan drippings to a skillet and heat over medium-high heat. Add a little olive oil if necessary.

2. Add aromatics like minced shallot, onion (red or yellow), scallion, or hardy herbs or spices to the skillet and cook, stirring often, until they are fragrant.

3. Deglaze the pan with some liquid. This could be stock or broth, beer, cider, wine (or mirin rice wine or vermouth), or sake. Bring the liquid to a simmer.

4. Reduce the heat to low and swirl in a pad of butter. Season with salt, pepper, and tender herbs (basil, dill, parsley, etc.). Add a splash of acid (lemon or lime juice, a drop or two of balsamic or a soft vinegar like sherry vinegar or rice vinegar), then pour over the meat and serve.

ARUGULA–HAZELNUT PESTO

Makes 2¹/₂ cups (enough to sauce 2 pounds of pasta)

1 cup blanched hazelnuts or walnut pieces

3 medium garlic cloves, roughly chopped

5 cups lightly packed arugula (about 5 ounces)

Leaves from 1 large sprig basil (optional)

1 teaspoon kosher salt

½ teaspoon freshly ground black pepper

1 cup extra-virgin olive oil

1 cup finely grated Parmigiano-Reggiano cheese

When I'm craving a bright, simple, clean, and green pesto but there aren't enough leaves on the basil plants in the garden, I make arugula pesto. The richness of the hazelnuts rounds out the arugula's peppery bite. I like to add the leaves from a sprig of basil if available to give just a hint of that classic pesto flavor. This recipe makes enough for 2 pounds of pasta, so use half now and refrigerate the rest in an airtight container (cover with a spare ¼" of oil to protect it from spoiling) for up to 1 week or freeze for a few months.

---

1 Add the nuts and garlic to the bowl of a food processor and pulse for three 1-second pulses to break them up and roughly grind.

2 Add the arugula, basil (if using), salt, and pepper. With the machine running, add the olive oil in a steady stream until the ingredients are well combined. Turn off the food processor, add the cheese, and pulse to combine.

3 Scrape the pesto into an airtight container and refrigerate until using.

Removing Skins from Hazelnuts

It's really convenient to buy already peeled hazelnuts, but they can sometimes be hard to find. The skins on hazelnuts are bitter, so it's good to remove them. Preheat the oven to 350°F and place the hazelnuts on a rimmed sheet pan. Toast them in the oven until they are just fragrant, 8 to 10 minutes. Immediately enclose the hazelnuts in a kitchen towel, and use the towel to rub them back and forth. The friction combined with the heat coming off the nuts removes the skin fairly easily.

MUSSELS MARINIÈRE *Serves 4*

4 tablespoons unsalted butter

4 medium garlic cloves, peeled and very thinly sliced

½ medium yellow onion, thinly sliced

1 piece (3" long) lemongrass, tough outer peel removed, tender stalk smashed with the side of a knife

2 dried makrut lime leaves

¼ teaspoon fine sea salt

¼ teaspoon freshly ground black pepper

1 cup dry white wine or vermouth

½ cup halved cherry tomatoes

2 pounds cleaned and debearded mussels (any mussels with broken shells discarded)

2 tablespoons mayonnaise

Finely grated zest and juice of 1 lemon

3 tablespoons finely chopped fresh flat-leaf parsley

Garlic Toasts
1 baguette, sliced on a diagonal into ⅓"- to ½"-thick pieces

3 garlic cloves, smashed

¼ cup mayonnaise

I used to *love* Anne of Green Gables, both the books and the PBS show. My sister and I would read the books feverishly, which all took place on Prince Edward Island in Canada. It was a kind of predecessor to *Downton Abbey* in a very early 1980s Victoriana/Laura Ashley kind of way and was hugely influential for me with all of the flowers, greenery, and chintz. So whenever I make mussels, of course I always try to buy ones from Prince Edward Island, which are known as PEI mussels. They're plump and juicy, and when served with pasta, they make a wonderfully delicious meal in hardly any time at all.

1   Melt 2 tablespoons of the butter in a large pot over medium-low heat. Add the garlic, onion, lemongrass, lime leaves, salt, and pepper and cook, stirring often, until the onion is very soft, about 10 minutes.

2   *To make the garlic toasts:* Meanwhile, rub one side of each piece of bread with the garlic. Spread some mayonnaise over the garlic-rubbed side of each piece of bread. Adjust an oven rack to the upper-middle position and heat the broiler to high. Set the bread on an aluminum foil–lined baking sheet and broil until toasted, 1½ to 2 minutes (watch the bread closely as broiler intensities vary!). Turn the bread slices over and lightly toast the other side, 30 seconds to 1 minute. Remove the bread from the oven and set aside.

3   Add the wine to the onion mixture, increase the heat to high, and bring to a boil. Reduce the heat to medium and simmer until the wine is reduced by half, 4 to 5 minutes.

4   Stir in the tomatoes, then add the mussels, cover the pot, and cook, shaking the pan occasionally, until the mussels open, 2 to 3 minutes. Use a slotted spoon to divide the opened mussels among four bowls. Add the remaining 2 tablespoons butter and the mayonnaise to the sauce and cook, stirring often, until the butter is melted, 30 seconds or so. Remove and discard the lemongrass and lime leaves as well as any mussels that haven't opened. Stir in the lemon zest, juice, and parsley, then divide the sauce over each bowl of mussels. Serve with the garlic toasts.

SMOKED BARBECUED RIBS *Serves 4*

Rib Rub

1½ teaspoons cumin seeds

1½ teaspoons fennel seeds

1½ teaspoons coarse brown sugar (such as turbinado or Demerara sugar/sugar in the raw)

1½ teaspoons coarse sea salt

1½ teaspoons whole black peppercorns

1 teaspoon dried oregano

½ teaspoon dried thyme

1 tablespoon sweet paprika

1 tablespoon onion powder

½ teaspoon chili powder

½ teaspoon ground cinnamon

½ teaspoon ground cloves

½ teaspoon ground ginger

½ teaspoon dried mustard

Ribs

2 slabs baby back pork ribs, membrane removed from the back of the ribs

2 cups your favorite barbecue sauce (like Sweet Baby Ray's—I like adding a few drops of liquid smoke for extra smokiness!)

My dad is from St. Louis, home not just to people who love barbecue but to people who *live* for barbecue. In fact, my dad is so committed that he agrees to travel to universities as a visiting artist only if the town has good barbecue. For his legendary ribs, he makes a spice blend, then smokes the ribs for nearly 3 hours before finishing them off over live fire. True to his St. Louis roots, the ribs get a baste of barbecue sauce at the end of grilling—sticky-sweet-spicy-smoky, he wouldn't have them any other way.

1 Heat your smoker to 150°F following the manufacturer's instructions.

2 *To make the rib rub:* Add the cumin seeds, fennel seeds, sugar, salt, peppercorns, oregano, and thyme to a spice grinder or coffee grinder and pulverize until finely ground. Add the paprika, onion powder, chili powder, cinnamon, cloves, ginger, and mustard and pulse to combine, then transfer to a small bowl.

3 *To make the ribs:* Rub the spices into both sides of the ribs and place the ribs on the grill rack, close the lid, and smoke them for 2 hours.

4 Increase the smoker temperature to 325°F. Transfer each slab to a large sheet of aluminum foil and tightly wrap them shut. Return the aluminum-wrapped slabs to the grill and cook until when you peek into the foil, the ends of the rib bones are white, the meat has shrunk, and the bones are exposed, about 45 minutes.

5 Unwrap the ribs and pour off any collected fat from the foil into the barbecue sauce, stirring to combine. Set the slabs meaty side up directly on the grill. Baste with the barbecue sauce and continue to grill until they look sticky and the meat falls off the bone with a gentle pull, 30 to 45 minutes. Transfer to a cutting board and use a sharp knife to separate the ribs. Pile the ribs on a platter and serve.

BEER CAN CHICKEN *Serves 4*

2 handfuls hickory wood chips

2 teaspoons fine sea salt

1 teaspoon ground cumin

1 teaspoon dried oregano

1 teaspoon freshly ground black pepper

1 chicken (4–5 pounds), rinsed inside and out and patted dry

2 tablespoons extra-virgin olive oil

1 can beer (your choice!)

1 small apple, pear, peach, or nectarine

I remember when my dad first started making beer can chicken. I was slightly horrified. I mean, the thought of sticking a beer can up the chicken just seemed very undignified! Once I tried the juicy, crisp-skinned, and incredibly tasty chicken, however, I came around. Who was I to take issue with how the poor chicken looked sitting on a can of beer? Fashion and flavor are so personal—there really are no rules. Through experimentation, be it recipes or looks, you can help form your means of expression that will define you as someone with your own style. You'll see in the recipe that the beer can is left half full with liquid to help steam the chicken from the inside. We are partial to using a dark beer, but, of course, you can use any kind you like—and if you're not into beer, you can make it using a can of soda or lemonade.

1 Place the wood chips in a bowl, cover with water, and soak for 30 minutes. Follow the manufacturer's instructions for heating a charcoal or gas grill to high heat. Bank the coals (or light the gas grill) so the heat is banked to the left and right sides with a cool spot in the middle. Set a drip pan in the middle between the coals (or heat sources), and then put the grill grate in place and let it heat up.

2 Mix the salt, cumin, oregano, and pepper together in a small bowl. Place the chicken on your work surface and rub inside the cavity and all over the skin with the olive oil. Rub 1 teaspoon of the spice blend inside the chicken. Gently wiggle your fingers under the skin of the breast to carefully separate the skin from the meat. Rub 3 teaspoons of the spice blend onto the breast meat.

3 Open the beer and pour out half (for yourself or whomever would enjoy it most!). Add the remaining spice blend to the beer in the can. Use a church key to create three more holes in the top of the beer can, then sit the chicken on top of the can, inserting the can into the cavity of the chicken so it sits upright. Place the apple in the neck opening to seal it shut.

4 Use a grill brush to scrape any residue off the grill grate, then carefully lift it up and scatter the drained wood chips on top of the coals (or divide them among two disposable trays or pieces of aluminum foil if using a gas grill). Return the grill grate to the grill and place the chicken on the grill grate over the drip pan so the wings are over the coals (or heat source)—the chicken should be pretty stable. Make sure the top and bottom vents are open on the grill, close the grill, and grill the chicken for 30 minutes.

5 Open the grill and give the chicken a quarter turn so the breast and backbone are over the charcoal (or heat source). Continue to cook, covered, until the skin is dark and crisp and an instant-read thermometer inserted into the leg/thigh joint reads 165°F and the juices run clear, about another 1 hour.

6 Remove the chicken from the grill (leave it on the beer can) and set aside for 15 minutes to rest. Using thick folded paper towels or pot holders, carefully lift the chicken off the beer can and discard the beer can (careful, the liquid inside the can is hot!) and the apple from the neck. Carve the chicken, arrange on a platter, and serve.

BUCKS COUNTY BLUEBERRY PIE *Makes one 9" pie or*

4 to 6 mini pies, depending on the size of the pie molds

1 recipe My Favorite
Pie Dough (page 50),
divided into 2 rounds
and chilled

½ cup granulated
sugar

¼ cup packed dark
brown sugar

3 tablespoons potato
starch or cornstarch

1 teaspoon ground
cinnamon

¼ teaspoon plus a
pinch of fine sea salt

4 cups (1 quart) fresh
blueberries

1 large egg, lightly
beaten

Sanding sugar,
for extra sparkle

Vanilla or almond ice
cream, for serving

On a family trip to Nova Scotia, I began a lifelong obsession with blueberry pie. I remember walking up sand dune cliffs to an archipelago stretching out to the sea where there were hundreds of white bunnies with long ears jumping around wild blueberry bushes. Does it get any more magical than that? Now when I get to pick blueberries in the summertime, I think back to that moment, and it always makes me smile. The best blueberry pie is made with the best blueberries, and the best blueberries are always the freshest, picked right off the bush. Save the frozen berries for pancakes and smoothies.

1 Roll one disk of pie dough between two sheets of parchment paper into a 10" circle that is between ⅛" to ¼" thick. Remove the top sheet of parchment (save both sheets of parchment for rolling the other dough round) and flip the dough over into a 9" pie plate. Fit the dough into the pie plate and remove the parchment. Place the pie plate in the refrigerator to chill while you roll out the second piece of dough. Leave the second piece between the sheets of parchment paper and slide it onto a flat surface in the fridge.

2 Adjust an oven rack to the bottom position and preheat the oven to 450°F. Whisk together the granulated sugar, brown sugar, potato starch, cinnamon, and ¼ teaspoon of the salt in a large bowl. Add the blueberries and toss to combine. Remove the pie crust from the fridge and add the berries to it.

3 Now you have a decorative choice: Make a lattice crust (see pages 48 and 49 for a visual) or go for a traditional top crust (lay the crust on top, trim the edges to within ½" of the pie plate rim, tuck under the overhang dough, and crimp as you like by pinching with your thumb and forefinger or pressing a design into the edge with the tines of a fork). You can also stamp shapes out of the second pie dough round using a cookie cutter (pages 48 and 49) and layer them over the berries.

4 Whisk the egg, 1 tablespoon of water, and a pinch of salt together in a small bowl. Brush the top of the crust with the egg wash and sprinkle with the sanding sugar. Set the pie on a rimmed baking sheet and place it on the bottom oven rack. Bake for 20 minutes, then reduce the oven temperature to 375°F and continue to bake until the top and bottom crust look browned and crisp, 35 to 45 minutes longer. Remove the pie from the oven and set aside for at least 30 minutes to let the blueberry filling set before slicing. Serve with a scoop of ice cream.

Make It Your Berry Best Pie

You could say I am a connoisseur of blueberry pie. I love it, I eat it, I bake it, I savor it and am always tinkering with my recipe (because really, that's what's so fun about cooking!). Here are some of my blueberry pie tips that have come after a lot of experimentation. You don't have to agree (but you'd be remiss not to!).

- Use only the freshest blueberries you can find. Don't make a pie with frozen berries. Don't make an out-of-season blueberry pie! Wait until you have perfect peak-season blueberries, and you'll be rewarded with the best pie of your life.

- Use potato starch instead of cornstarch for a more jelly-like set. And don't skip the starch, because otherwise your pie will be more like blueberry soup than pie!

- Save the lemons for lemonade! Blueberries, especially fresh ones from a local farm, have lots of balanced acidity. You really don't need the lemon juice.

- If you like a clean slice of pie, use a lattice crust (see pages 48 and 49). This allows more liquid in the pie to evaporate during baking. If you like blueberry pie that oozes out the sides and gets served in a bowl (topped with vanilla ice cream, of course), then go for a traditional double crust.

MY FAVORITE PIE
DOUGH *Makes enough dough for 1 double-crusted*
9¹/₂" pie or 2 single-crust pies (or tarts)

**1 cup (2 sticks)
unsalted butter**

**2½ cups all-purpose
flour**

**1 teaspoon granulated
sugar**

**1½ teaspoons fine
sea salt**

2 large egg yolks

A food processor makes the job easy, but you could also make pie dough by hand pressing the butter into the flour using your fingers. For a flaky crust, use cold ingredients; I always freeze the butter for 15 minutes before using it, which helps to create the flakiest crust.

1 Cut the butter into ½" pieces and place them on a plate. Freeze the butter for 15 minutes while you get the rest of the pie ingredients together. Fill a measuring cup with ½ cup of water and a few ice cubes and set aside.

2 Add the flour, sugar, and salt to the bowl of a food processor fitted with the metal blade and pulse to combine. Add the cold butter and pulse the mixture together until the butter is in small yellow pieces no bigger than a very tiny pebble, about 15 to 20 one-second pulses. Add the egg yolks and pulse 4 to 5 times, until the flour mixture starts to clump. Add 5 tablespoons of ice water to the food processor and pulse it in until the mixture starts to ride up the sides of the processor's bowl, 4 to 5 one-second pulses.

3 Remove the top of the food processor and squeeze some of the dough in your hand. When you open your hand, the dough should hold together nicely without dry spots, and when pressed, it should flake apart nicely (without being too crumbly and dry). If the dough doesn't do this, add 1 more tablespoon of ice water to the mixture, replace the lid, and pulse twice to combine.

4 Place a long sheet of plastic wrap on your work surface and turn out half of the dough into the center of the plastic. Wrap the edges of the plastic wrap around the dough and then flatten and massage the dough into a ½"- to ¾"-thick circle. Wrap the dough tightly in plastic and repeat with the remaining dough in a separate piece of plastic. Refrigerate for at least 30 minutes before using, or up to 3 days. Or place the dough in a resealable freezer bag and freeze for up to 3 months. Defrost in the refrigerator overnight before using.

STRAWBERRY–RHUBARB TARTLETS *Makes 8 tartlets*

1 tablespoon
unsalted butter, plus
1 tablespoon, melted,
for greasing the tart
molds

1 sheet all-butter
puff pastry (thawed
if frozen)

½ pound rhubarb
stalks (2–3 large
stalks), sliced into
½" pieces on the bias
(about 2 cups)

½ cup granulated
sugar

2 tablespoons fresh
lemon juice (from
about ½ lemon)

1 teaspoon finely
grated orange zest,
plus 2 tablespoons
fresh orange juice
(from about ¼ orange)

⅛ teaspoon plus a
pinch of fine sea salt

2 cups (1 pint)
strawberries, hulled
and halved or
quartered if large
(about 2 cups; set 8 of
the smallest and most
perfect strawberries
aside for decorating)

1½ teaspoons
cornstarch

1 large egg

Coarse sugar (such as
Demerara or sanding
sugar), for sprinkling

Whipped cream or
crème fraîche, for
serving

Rhubarb was a surprise on the farm in Bucks County, Pennsylvania. We didn't plant it; it was surely put in by the farmer before us. The stunning and lanky fuchsia stems popped up in the early spring, and I baked them in tarts and pies and even pickled them—there always seems to be more than I know what to do with. It is kind of a tropical-looking plant with big palm–like leaves (but don't eat the leaves—they're poisonous!). Slicing rhubarb on a bias helps reduce its stringiness; it's similar to celery in that way. For the tart crust, decorative scissors from the craft store are fantastic for cutting the dough into shapes with fun edges. Zigzag scissors are my favorite!

1 Brush eight 3"- to 3½"-wide mini fluted brioche molds with the melted butter (or lightly mist with nonstick cooking spray; if you don't have fluted brioche molds, you can use a muffin pan—just leave the four remaining cups empty since the recipe makes only eight tartlets). Set the puff pastry on your work surface and cut it into eight 4" squares. Use a fork to prick each square all over, then fit each one into the prepared brioche molds (or muffin pan), letting the corners stand up above the rim. Place the molds in the refrigerator to chill (setting them on a sheet pan is easiest as long as your refrigerator can accommodate the size of the pan). Adjust an oven rack to the lowest position and preheat the oven to 400°F.

2 Cut the remaining puff pastry dough and dough scraps into uneven strips (for creating artistic lattice) or use a cookie cutter to stamp out decorative shapes—leaves, stars, and circles are all pretty. Place the pastry cutouts on a parchment paper–lined baking sheet. Use a fork to prick the pieces all over and then refrigerate them to chill before baking.

3 Melt the remaining 1 tablespoon of butter in a medium saucepan over medium heat. Add the rhubarb, granulated sugar, lemon juice, orange zest, all but 1 teaspoon of the

recipe continues

orange juice, and $\frac{1}{8}$ teaspoon of the salt and cook, stirring occasionally, until the rhubarb releases some liquid and the liquid comes to a simmer, about 5 minutes. Add the strawberries and cook until they begin to just soften, about 2 minutes, stirring occasionally. Add the cornstarch to a small bowl and stir in the remaining 1 teaspoon of orange juice, then scrape the mixture into the pan with the rhubarb. Continue to cook, stirring once or twice, until a few bubbles burst at the surface, 1 to 2 minutes. Turn off the heat and set the strawberry-rhubarb mixture aside to cool (you should have about 2 cups).

4 Remove the dough-lined brioche molds from the refrigerator and line each with a 5" square of aluminum foil or parchment paper. Add enough pie weights or dry beans to each tart to fill the mold halfway. Place the tart shells on a baking sheet (if they aren't already) and bake on the bottom oven rack until the edges turn golden brown, 17 to 19 minutes. Remove the baking sheet from the oven and set the tartlets aside to cool for 5 minutes before carefully lifting out the liner and weights from each shell.

5 Whisk the egg with 1 tablespoon of water and a pinch of salt in a small bowl. Divide the cooled strawberry-rhubarb filling among each tart shell (it should fill the shell about three-quarters of the way up the sides). Set the pastry strips or shapes on a parchment paper–lined rimmed baking sheet. Brush the tops and edges of the tartlets with the egg wash and sprinkle with coarse sugar, then do the same with the pastry strips or cutout shapes.

6 Reduce the oven temperature to 375°F. Return the tartlets to the oven. Place the sheet pan with the decorative shapes in the oven as well and bake until the pastry is golden brown, 18 to 20 minutes for the decorative pieces and 25 to 30 minutes for the tarts (the filling should bubble around the edges of the pastry). Set the decorative pieces of pastry on a wire rack to cool and let the tartlets cool completely before popping them out of the molds (use a knife to loosen the pastry from the pan if needed). Thinly slice the reserved strawberries (if they are large; if they're cute and tiny, you can leave them whole) and arrange them on top of each tartlet along with the decorative cutouts before serving with whipped cream or crème fraîche.

CHARLOTTE AUX FRAMBOISES *Serves 8*

1¾ cups plus
2 tablespoons
granulated sugar

2 pints (4 cups) fresh
raspberries (or 3 cups
frozen raspberries
and 1 cup fresh
raspberries)

½ teaspoon fresh
lemon juice

2 large egg yolks

1 tablespoon vanilla
extract

1 pint (2 cups) heavy
cream

1 package (about
2½ teaspoons)
granulated gelatin

1 package (7 ounces)
ladyfinger cookies

With its ladyfinger perimeter, pale pink and creamy raspberry filling, and bright, sweet raspberry gelée on top, it's a shamelessly pretty composition that is like a ball gown made of Chantilly lace and tulle—so wonderfully nostalgic and 1950s classic. I only make it on request for special occasions like my mom's birthday.

1 Make the raspberry cream: Bring 1¼ cups of the sugar and 1¼ cups of water to a simmer in a medium saucepan set over medium-high heat. Stir until the sugar is dissolved, then add 3 cups of the raspberries. Reduce the heat to medium-low and gently simmer until the mixture is thickened, about 15 minutes, stirring occasionally. Stir in the lemon juice. Strain the raspberry mixture through a fine-mesh sieve and into a medium bowl, pressing on the seeds and solids to extract as much liquid as possible. Pour ¾ cup of the raspberry sauce into a medium bowl and set aside.

2 Whisk the egg yolks, ½ cup of the sugar, and the vanilla together in a medium heat-safe bowl. Heat 1 cup of the cream in a small saucepan set over medium heat until it comes to a simmer. Whisk the warm cream into the egg mixture a little at a time until the bottom of the bowl is warm. Once it is all added, pour it back into the saucepan (the one you used to warm the cream).

3 Set the saucepan over medium-low heat and cook, stirring constantly, until the custard thickens and leaves a trail on the back of a wooden spoon (dip the spoon into the custard, remove it, and use your finger to draw a line—if the line doesn't run and stays clear, the custard is done). Immediately pour the custard through a fine-mesh sieve and into a clean medium bowl. Stir in the remaining raspberry sauce (not the reserved ¾ cup) and set the raspberry custard aside to cool.

recipe continues

4 Add ½ cup of cold water to a small heat-safe bowl. Sprinkle the gelatin over the top and set it aside for 5 minutes to soften. Place the bowl in the microwave and heat for 30 seconds to liquefy the gelatin mixture, then stir half of it into the raspberry custard and the other half into the ¾ cup of reserved raspberry sauce. Cover the bowl of raspberry custard with plastic wrap and refrigerate while you prepare the pan.

5 Set a 9" springform pan on top of a piece of parchment or waxed paper and trace a circle around the pan. Cut out the circle and set it into the bottom of the pan. Cut one end off of each ladyfinger so it has a flat edge to stand on and so the rounded opposite end is more or less the same height as the pan. Stand the ladyfinger up in the pan with the flat side facing the interior and the rounded side facing the springform ring. Repeat with enough ladyfingers to make a ring around the entire springform mold.

6 Remove the raspberry custard from the refrigerator and discard the plastic wrap. Pour the remaining 1 cup of cream into the bowl of a stand mixer (or large bowl if beating by hand) fitted with the whisk attachment and beat on medium-high speed with the remaining 2 tablespoons of sugar until the cream holds stiff peaks, 1½ to 2 minutes. Whisk the whipped cream into the raspberry cream, then add half of it to the springform mold, being careful not to disturb the ladyfinger perimeter. Sprinkle the remaining 1 cup of raspberries over the raspberry cream and cover with the remaining raspberry cream. Pour the reserved raspberry sauce over the top of the charlotte (if it has set up, gently warm it by setting it over a bowl of hot water until the sauce liquefies).

7 Cover the top of the pan with plastic wrap and refrigerate for at least 2 hours or overnight. The next day, remove and discard the plastic wrap and place the pan on a cake plate. Unclasp the mold and carefully lift it off the charlotte. Present to your guests and slice tableside.

BLUEBERRY BLONDIES

Makes 9 blondies

½ cup (1 stick) plus
1 tablespoon unsalted
butter, at room
temperature

1 cup plus
2 tablespoons
all-purpose flour

¼ teaspoon baking
soda

¼ teaspoon fine
sea salt

½ cup roasted
pistachios, roughly
chopped

¾ cup lightly packed
light brown sugar

Finely grated zest
of ½ orange

1 large egg

1 shot espresso (or
3 tablespoons strong
brewed coffee)

1 teaspoon vanilla
extract

¼ teaspoon almond
extract

½ cup dried
blueberries

My nephew Cyrus doesn't like chocolate or pizza—you might say that he marches to his own drummer! So when my sister brings her kids out to the country house for the weekend, I aim to please and make these blondie bar cookies. They are tender, buttery, and sweet, and instead of chocolate chips, I use dried blueberries, which, when combined with pistachios and orange zest, make the bars super sophisticated yet still decadent in all the right ways. Think a chocolate chip cookie that is ever so slightly healthier!

1   Preheat the oven to 375°F. Lightly coat a 9" x 9" baking dish or pan with 1 tablespoon of the butter and set aside.

2   Whisk together the flour, baking soda, and salt in a medium bowl. Whisk in the pistachios and set aside.

3   Add the brown sugar and orange zest to the bowl of a stand mixer fitted with the paddle attachment. Use your fingers to rub the zest into the sugar until the sugar is fragrant. Add the remaining ½ cup of butter to the sugar and mix on medium-low speed until combined. Increase the mixer speed to medium-high and beat until creamy and airy, about 2 minutes.

4   Reduce the speed to medium and add the egg, mixing well and scraping the bottom and sides of the bowl as needed. Add the espresso, vanilla, and almond extract and beat until incorporated.

5   Reduce the speed to medium-low and add the blueberries, then add the dry ingredients and mix until just combined. Use a rubber spatula to spread the blondie batter in the prepared pan, spreading it out evenly. Bake until the blondies are golden brown and spring back when pressed, and a cake tester inserted into the center comes out clean, 18 to 20 minutes. Remove from the oven and cool completely before slicing into nine 3" x 3" squares and serving.

STRAWBERRY–MINT ICE CREAM *Makes 1 quart*

2 cups heavy cream

1 cup whole milk

1 cup granulated sugar

Pinch of fine sea salt

¼ cup packed fresh mint leaves, plus ¼ cup finely chopped mint leaves

6 large egg yolks

1 vanilla bean, split lengthwise down the center

1 quart (4 cups) fresh strawberries

Grated zest of 1 lemon, plus 2 teaspoons lemon juice

It's not summertime to me until I have my first bowl of home-churned strawberry ice cream. You have to wait until strawberries are at their peak, which in the Northeast is in early July. Eating these ripe strawberries that you get from farm stands or u-picks is like gobbling baby spoonfuls of jam—so naturally sweet and wonderful. I love the flavor of real mint with strawberries, but I advise against using spearmint since its flavor is too assertive for strawberries. Better to go with a subtle peppermint instead.

1 Bring the cream, milk, ⅔ cup of the sugar, and the salt to a strong simmer over medium-high heat in a medium saucepan. Turn off the heat and add the whole mint leaves. Cover the pan and let the mint steep for 15 minutes, then use a slotted spoon to remove the mint leaves, pressing on them to extract all the liquid.

2 Lightly beat the yolks in a medium bowl. Return the cream mixture to a simmer. Turn off the heat and drizzle about 2 tablespoons of the cream mixture into the yolks. Whisk well, then continue to add more of the cream mixture, a few tablespoons at a time, until the bottom of the bowl that the yolks are in is warm. Pour the yolk mixture into the saucepan with the remaining cream.

3 Set the saucepan over medium heat and cook the mixture slowly, stirring constantly with a wooden spoon and making sure to get into the edges of the pan and across the bottom, until the mixture thickens slightly (when you take the wooden spoon out of the mixture, use your finger to draw a straight line across the spoon; if the line holds and doesn't run together, the mixture is ready).

4 Strain the custard through a fine-mesh sieve and into a medium bowl to remove any lumps. Use the tip of a paring knife to scrape the vanilla seeds out of the bean and add them

to the custard (save the bean and add it to a jar of granulated sugar to infuse it with vanilla essence), whisking to combine. Cover the bowl with plastic wrap and refrigerate overnight. Chill the bowl for your ice cream maker, too, if that is what the manufacturer recommends.

5 The next day, hull and halve the strawberries. Combine them with the remaining ⅓ cup of sugar, the lemon zest, and lemon juice in a blender or food processor (or in a medium bowl if using an immersion blender). Purée until well combined.

6 Follow the ice cream maker's instructions to churn the chilled mint base. Once the base looks like soft serve ice cream, add the puréed strawberries and the chopped mint. Continue to churn for another minute or two to combine. Transfer the ice cream to an airtight container and freeze for at least 1½ hours or overnight before scooping and serving.

Conscientious Mint Tactics

Mint is an aggressive herb. In fact, most gardeners actually consider it a weed because it simply spreads and spreads and can overwhelm more sensitive and tender plants. That's why I like to plant mint in its own restricted environment, be it a terra-cotta pot, a galvanized steel trough, or its own little dirt bed. Happy plants make for a happy garden!

RESORT

While I am working on my Resort Collection and well before it reaches the stores in early fall, I keep in mind the sound of the ocean and the feeling of the sand because I want that feeling to come through in the clothing that people purchase for their getaways. There's something exciting and perhaps unfamiliar in each of these recipes, with my goal being to re-create that moment when you step off a plane for a vacation and you're filled with happiness and anticipation—and you're so ready for that first dip in the water.

I have been seeking the perfect midwinter getaway forever. Of course, it's not just what the place has to offer me from a sun and fun standpoint but from a food perspective as well—because for me, a big part of rest and relaxation is cooking and eating. I went to the Yucatán before it became so developed, when it was still wild and a little bohemian. I climbed over the Mayan ruins at Coba outside of Tulum—well before Tulum was discovered by yoga lovers. I also loved going to St. Maarten with my mom, who was there on business. We explored the Dutch and French sides of the island, enjoying all the great culinary fusions the island has to offer, like Dutch *rijsttafel* (an Indonesian feast of satay, rice dishes, and sambals, among other small plates) and fresh local grilled fish. From a food perspective, one of my favorite places for an escape is Harbour Island in the Bahamas. It is a very simple place where I can bring my dogs, shop at local markets, cook, and entertain. I really love zipping around in the golf carts as few cars are allowed there—talk about a change of pace from my atelier on Fifth Avenue in New York City!

Through travel I have enjoyed many wonderful cuisines of the world, from the Mediterranean to far Asia and South America. The dishes in this chapter are, for the most part, fresh and healthy, high on vegetables and low on fat, because when I'm traveling and taking some time to take care of my health, mind, and soul, that's what I like to eat. So maybe you can't get to the Bahamas, Kyoto, or the Amalfi coast, but you *can* cook up something delicious to bring your senses there.

The Resort Collection is a perfect precursor to the pre-fall collection that bridges summer and fall. This is that "in-between season," a shoulder season of sorts, where you begin to feel a crisp autumnal coolness in the air upon waking up, but by noon the sun is beaming just as brilliantly as it does in August. For all of us in the fashion world, this moment begins when Fashion Week takes over New York City in early September. Because my work is so hectic and intense leading up to September, it's important to keep my health and stamina up by eating as many fresh fruits, vegetables, lean proteins, and long-lasting carbohydrates as I can. When I'm spending long days in the atelier getting my Fall Collection ready for the runway, I like to come home to simple, fresh, and quick foods to prepare like salads, pasta with fresh vegetables, and even scrambled eggs for dinner. I know the growing season is short and fleeting, soon to give way to colder temperatures and the heartier vegetables, stews, and richer preparations that mark the traditional fall season, so now is the time to overwhelm myself with the last round of leafy greens before they go to seed, the final flush of tomatoes, and the few peppers and chiles that remain to twist off the vine.

RESORT

GEORGE V SCRAMBLED EGGS *Serves 4*

9 large eggs

¾ cup heavy cream or half-and-half (or whole milk in a pinch)

1 tablespoon finely chopped fresh herbs (such as dill, parsley, rosemary, thyme)

¾ teaspoon sea salt

½ teaspoon freshly ground black pepper

2 tablespoons unsalted butter

The *best* scrambled eggs I've ever had were at the luxurious Hotel George V in Paris, where I stayed with my friend Lola Schnabel, who had been invited by John Galliano to see the Dior show in Paris. I had never stayed in such a grand and glamorous hotel. For breakfast I ordered the scrambled eggs, and they were so custardy and light that they were nothing short of an absolute revelation. I learned that it's important to cook them in a double boiler so the eggs cook slowly, allowing for lots of stirring to create soft curds (if you don't have a double boiler, cook the eggs in a nonstick skillet set over a saucepan of simmering water—I've done this and it works!). I also learned that for the creamiest Parisian-style scramble, it is essential to use only cream and butter in the eggs, with some fresh chopped herbs, of course.

1 Whisk together the eggs, cream, herbs, salt, and pepper in a medium bowl.

2 Heat 1" of water in a medium saucepan over medium-high heat. Once it comes to a simmer, reduce the heat to medium and set a medium nonstick skillet over the saucepan. Let the skillet warm up for 1 minute (if the water is boiling too hard in the saucepan, reduce the heat to medium-low or low). Add the butter to the skillet, and once it melts, add the egg mixture.

3 Use a rubber spatula to slowly stir the eggs. After a few minutes, the eggs will begin to set and form small, creamy curds. Continue to slowly stir until the eggs are no longer raw and watery but are set and creamy, 4 to 5 minutes. Taste and add more salt if needed. Divide among plates and serve.

FRENCH TOAST WITH FRESH BERRY SYRUP *Serves 4*

French Toast

4 large eggs

1 cup heavy cream

¼ cup granulated sugar

1 tablespoon ground cinnamon

1 teaspoon vanilla extract

Pinch of sea salt

2 tablespoons unsalted butter

1 loaf day-old challah bread (or 2 or 3 days old), cut into ¾"-thick slices (you want at least 8 slices)

Powdered sugar, for serving

Berry Syrup

¾ cup maple syrup

1 cup fresh berries, halved if large (blackberries, blueberries, raspberries, strawberries)

On Friday afternoons, my favorite thing to do is hop in a car with Tina, my miniature poodle, and get on my way to the country house in Pennsylvania. En route to the tunnel out of Manhattan, I always stop at a great bakery in lower Manhattan to buy lots of good bread for the weekend. I'll get a seeded loaf, perhaps a baguette for car snacking (and yes, maybe a croissant, too), and most often a loaf of challah bread for weekend French toast. By Sunday, the challah is perfectly semi-stale to soak up a quick custard that permeates to the core so that it tastes wonderfully rich and eggy but not soggy. I add fresh berries (or frozen from the summer harvest) to maple syrup for a very fast and flavorful berry syrup that makes the French toast taste that much more special and delicious.

---

1 *To make the French toast:* Whisk the eggs, cream, granulated sugar, cinnamon, vanilla, and salt together in a medium bowl.

2 Melt ½ tablespoon of the butter in a large nonstick skillet over medium-high heat. Add a slice of challah to the egg mixture and saturate both sides. Let the excess drip back into the bowl and add the challah to the pan. Repeat with one or two more slices of bread (don't overcrowd the pan—you want each slice to have enough room to lie flat). Reduce the heat to medium and cook until the challah is nicely browned on the bottom, 3 to 4 minutes. Use a spatula to flip the slices over and cook on the other side until browned, 2 to 3 minutes. Transfer to a platter.

3 Add ½ tablespoon of the butter to the pan and a few more slices of soaked challah. Repeat until all of the challah is browned (you may not use all of the butter).

recipe continues

4 *To make the berry syrup:* Meanwhile, add the maple syrup and berries to a small saucepan and warm over medium heat. Gently simmer until the berries break apart and the maple syrup takes on a berry-colored tint, 3 to 5 minutes. Turn off the heat.

5 Sprinkle powdered sugar over the French toast. Pour the syrup into a small pitcher and serve alongside the French toast.

Challah versus Brioche

Challah and brioche are both enriched breads, challah being traditionally a "Jewish" holiday bread and brioche being a French bread. Brioche is more buttery than challah, which can be made with butter but is often made with oil to keep it kosher. Both are fantastic in bread pudding (see Chocolate Croissant Bread Pudding on page 246; you can use either bread in place of the croissants), but are both equally as good in French toast? One Sunday morning, I put the two to the test in the country kitchen, serving up the pan-browned French toast to my parents. The brioche French toast was extra custardy but almost too soft and mushy, while the challah French toast kept some of its texture and had a nice custardy yet springy bite. In the Posen house, French toast will always be made with challah. What about in yours?

MIZUNA AND AVOCADO SALAD WITH CREAMY CASHEW–GINGER DRESSING *Serves 4*

¼ cup raw cashews

⅓ cup extra-virgin olive oil

¾ cup rice vinegar

1 scallion, finely chopped

1 shiso leaf, finely chopped (optional), or 1 tablespoon finely chopped cilantro or fresh Thai basil

1 teaspoon finely chopped fresh gingerroot

1 tablespoon mirin rice wine

1 teaspoon yuzu juice or fresh lemon juice

Pinch of sea salt

1 bunch mizuna greens (about 8 cups)

2 kyuri (Japanese) cucumbers, sliced on a bias into ¼"-thick pieces (or 3 Persian cucumbers or ½ English cucumber)

1 pint (2 cups) grape tomatoes, halved

1 Hass avocado, halved, pitted, peeled, and chopped

I have been going to the Japanese restaurant Japonica just north of Washington Square for birthdays and celebrations forever. Here I always feel at home, always lovingly welcomed by the staff and owners and integrated into the experience of a meal. The restaurant is decorated in a totally whimsical Japanese style that changes with every season. What began as a love of Japanese food has evolved into a lifelong interest in and appreciation for Japanese arts, crafts, culture, and design—and, of course, the food!

1   Place the cashews, olive oil, vinegar, scallion, shiso (if using), ginger, mirin, yuzu, and salt in a blender and process until smooth. If the dressing is very thick, add water 1 tablespoon at a time (you can add up to 3 tablespoons of water without dramatically softening the flavor) until the dressing reaches the desired consistency.

2   Arrange the mizuna, cucumbers, tomatoes, and avocado on a platter and drizzle the dressing over the top. Serve immediately.

A Web Site to Note

A great way to get to know Japanese cuisine, cooking, ingredients, technique, and culture is to check out the Web site for NHK World, Japan's public broadcasting organization (their version of PBS!). Here you can find hundreds of recipes and videos, all in English—finding NHK online was a revelation to me, and now I'm completely addicted!

¾ pound sushi-grade tuna

2 tablespoons ponzu sauce

1½ teaspoons apple cider vinegar

1½ teaspoons Dijon mustard

2 teaspoons brine-packed capers, drained and finely chopped

Scant 1 teaspoon freshly grated gingerroot

¼ teaspoon fine sea salt

¼ teaspoon freshly ground black pepper

⅛ teaspoon granulated sugar

1 tablespoon extra-virgin olive oil

1 teaspoon toasted sesame oil

2 scallions, very finely chopped

1 Persian cucumber or 1 small Kirby cucumber, halved, seeded, and finely chopped

½ small orange bell pepper, seeded and very finely chopped

½ small white onion or Vidalia onion, very finely chopped

¼ cup very finely chopped fennel (optional)

2 tablespoons finely chopped fresh dill

2 tablespoons finely chopped fresh flat-leaf parsley

1 small avocado, halved, pitted, peeled, and finely chopped

Black sesame seeds, for serving

TUNA TARTARE *Serves 4*

When I fly to Los Angeles, which I do several times a year for award shows or just to visit friends, my very first stop off the plane is usually the Polo Lounge at the Beverly Hills Hotel, where I take absolute delight in their steak tartare. However, I use tuna instead of beef as a great way to introduce the concept and flavors of tartare to friends, since some people do not like the idea of eating raw beef. This is one of my favorite vacation dishes because it's quick to prepare and feels so healthy and clean to eat.

1 Place the tuna on a cutting board and, using a very sharp knife, slice it against the grain into ¼" to ⅛" pieces. Stack a few pieces and slice them crosswise into ¼" to ⅛" pieces, then turn and slice again so you end up with ¼" to ⅛" cubes. Run your fingers through the tuna to break up any stringy pieces, then transfer it to a medium bowl and refrigerate.

2 Whisk together the ponzu sauce, vinegar, mustard, capers, ginger, salt, black pepper, and sugar in a large bowl. Add the olive oil and sesame oil and whisk until emulsified.

3 To the dressing, add the scallions, cucumber, bell pepper, onion, fennel (if using), dill, and parsley and stir to combine. Add the cold tuna and use your fingers to toss the mixture, then add the avocado and gently toss the tartare one more time.

4 Divide among four plates, sprinkle with the sesame seeds, and serve immediately.

VARIATION: TUNA TARTARE HAND ROLLS

Lay a piece of butter leaf lettuce or red leaf lettuce on a cutting board. Place 1 to 2 tablespoons of the tartare within the lettuce leaf and roll it to enclose the mixture.

VARIATION: TUNA SASHIMI SALAD

Instead of chopping the tuna in step 1, thinly slice it into ⅛"-thick planks. Divide the tuna among four plates. Toss the vegetables with the ponzu–sesame oil sauce and add some over each serving of tuna.

The Best Tartare: It's All in the Details

Check off these three important must-haves for tuna tartare that can rival any you might find in a restaurant.

1. Make sure you can find the freshest and most beautiful tuna fillet available. I look for pieces without too much separation in the grain.

2. Use a freshly sharpened chef's knife for chopping the tuna. If the knife is dull, the tuna will become mushy and mealy, which will completely change the look and bite of the dish.

3. It's very important that all of the vegetables are very finely cut into small bits that are more or less equal in size. Use a sharp knife (see tip 2!) and take care in chopping to ensure your tartare looks beautiful and tastes great.

DINNER WITH YOHJI

Some years ago I met a wonderful jewelry designer, Justin Davis, who had lived in Tokyo for years and headed a luxury jewelry brand that was "rock and royal." He told me he entered into a design collaboration and bromance with the legend and national treasure of Japan, the designer Yohji Yamamoto. Yohji was introduced to my work through Justin, and because I am such a fan of Yohji's work, a casual get-together at Justin's home in Tokyo was arranged so we could meet one another. Justin was living in the former apartment of filmmaker Akira Kurosawa (whose film *The Hidden Fortress* is said to have inspired *Star Wars*). The place was palatial by Tokyo standards, with its big rooms and terrace overlooking the city at the very top of the building. When I arrived, no food was to be seen. And there was no Yohji to be seen either among the sea of punk rock and pop culture paraphernalia Justin had amassed. Then the doorbell rang and the most elegant older woman arrived carrying beautifully wrapped packages and boxes of the most exquisite sushi and sashimi that I had ever seen. She laid out a beautiful meal—including glowing orange uni, translucent kampachi, and perfect prawns that resembled mini lobsters. She turned to me and explained that her son, Yohji, would be on his way shortly. Dinner with Yohji and Justin was phenomenal (I learned never to dip rice into the soy sauce, rather delicately dip the fish upside down into the sauce). The meal came to an end, and I discovered that behind one of the most serious innovators in fashion was a warm, generous person with a witty, wicked sense of humor.

"Then the doorbell rang . . ."

BLOOD ORANGE AND FENNEL SALAD WITH ROSE WATER VINAIGRETTE *Serves 4*

4 blood oranges

Juice of 1 lemon

1 tablespoon best-quality rose water

1 tablespoon white wine vinegar or apple cider vinegar

1½ teaspoons Dijon mustard

½ teaspoon fine sea salt

¼ teaspoon freshly ground black pepper

¼ cup extra-virgin olive oil

1 medium head frisée, leaves removed from the root

1 bunch watercress, root end and any tough stems removed

1 large fennel bulb, halved, cored, and very thinly sliced using the slicer attachment on a food processor or a mandoline

Floral and aromatic, rose petals are distilled with steam to make rose water, an ingredient used for centuries in the Levant, northern Africa, India, and the Middle East. In this salad, rose water melds with the sweet-tart-bitter flavor of blood oranges and the licorice taste of fennel to create a salad that is all about fresh, bright, and intoxicating flavors. When I crave a getaway but can't logistically make it happen, this is the salad that gets me there, even if only for a few minutes.

1 Slice a thin sliver off of the top and bottom of one of the oranges to expose the fruit. Slice the peel and white pith off the fruit from top to bottom, turning the orange as you go. Hold the orange over a large bowl and use a sharp knife to slice along the side of each membrane, releasing the segments of orange into the bowl. Repeat with the remaining oranges.

2 Whisk together the lemon juice, rose water, vinegar, mustard, salt, and pepper in a small bowl. While whisking, slowly drizzle in the olive oil until all of the oil is added and the vinaigrette is thick and creamy (you can also add all of the vinaigrette ingredients to a Mason jar, fasten the lid, and shake it vigorously to emulsify the dressing).

3 Add the frisée, watercress, and fennel to the orange. Drizzle the dressing over the top and use your hands to gently toss everything together and coat all of the greens and oranges with the vinaigrette. Transfer to a salad bowl and serve.

EVERYTHING IS COMING UP ROSES

Nothing seems more wasteful than having gorgeous ingredients in my pantry and not using them! If you buy rose water especially to make the Blood Orange and Fennel Salad with Rose Water Vinaigrette, then please find other ways to use it in your everyday cooking. Here are some of my favorites:

- Add a few drops to a tropical fruit smoothie
- Make a rose water simple syrup for cocktails or add a few drops to champagne
- Whisk with citrus juice to toss with a fruit salad
- Sprinkle over ripe melon or strawberries
- Add a splash to a rice pilaf with dried fruit
- Use instead of vanilla in pound cake, waffles, buttercream, lemon scones, shortbread, or sugar cookies (page 125)
- And last but certainly not least, you can use rose water as a refresher for your skin!

GETTING TO KNOW YUZU
AND OTHER GREAT FLAVORS

In addition to saltiness, sweetness, bitterness, and sourness, the fifth basic taste is umami, which means "delicious" in Japanese (which makes sense because the fifth sense was discovered by a Japanese scientist). Umami translates as "savory" when describing this taste, which is used to wonderful effect in Japanese cooking.

There might be more than a few ingredients in some of the recipes in this book that you've never heard of before—mizuna, shiso, yuzu, mirin . . . trust me, though, they are all worth getting to know. Here are some ingredient CliffNotes, but really, nothing beats firsthand sampling. Find an Asian market near you and take joy in the feeling of discovery and curiosity, being surrounded by ingredients unknown to you, all with labels written in a different language. Don't feel overwhelmed or intimidated by the experience. You can always ask someone for help *or* just spend a few dollars and have a culinary adventure. There are also plenty of online sources that carry these items so you can have the best of Japan sent straight to your doorstep.

Bonito Flakes: Called *katusuobushi* in Japanese, bonito flakes are very thin dried, fermented, and smoked petal-like flakes of tuna or mackerel; they're one of the main ingredients used to make dashi.

Dashi: A stock made from kombu and bonito that's slow simmered and then strained; use it for miso soup, for steaming vegetables, or for making a pan sauce.

Furikake: A seasoning sprinkle often used over steamed sushi rice, fish, or vegetables. It is made with toasted sesame seeds, seaweed, and salt. Sometimes bonito flakes or dried shiso leaves are added.

Kombu: A wide, thick, dried edible kelp seaweed and a necessary ingredient for dashi. (I also like to add a piece to dried beans as they simmer and soften.) Kombu is a good source of glutamic acid, the amino acid responsible for umami.

Kyuri: Long and thin Japanese cucumbers that have very thin skins, no seeds, and a naturally sweet flavor.

Mirin: Similar to sake, mirin is a sweet, fermented rice wine that is used as a condiment and ingredient in dipping sauces and dressings.

Miso: Fermented soybean paste that is a little salty and offers dishes like soups, dressings, marinades, and glazes loads of umami flavor. White miso is the mellowest tasting, while red miso is the most robust. It can be fermented with a host of ingredients including barley, rice, wheat, buckwheat, quinoa, and even hemp seeds.

Mitsuba: A large-leaf Japanese parsley that tastes like a cross between anisey chervil, celery, and parsley.

Mizuna: A bitter green similar to arugula with an appearance like dandelion greens. Great in salads.

Myoga: Edible flower buds of Japanese ginger; thinly slice them lengthwise or mince and use as an herb/condiment or pickle.

Shichimi: A Japanese chile-based seasoning that is sprinkled over rice or soup and often contains seven ingredients including several types of chiles, dried orange peel, seaweed, sesame seeds, and ginger. Poppy seed, hemp seed, yuzu, and dried shiso leaves can also be added.

Shisito: A small, crinkly green chile pepper that is often blistered in a very hot pan and sprinkled with salt before serving. They are generally mild, but occasionally you'll get a spicy one!

Shiso: An herb with a wonderfully citrus-herbaceous taste that is somewhere between basil, mint, lime zest, and fresh orange. It is also sometimes called perilla.

Soba: Spaghetti-like strands of pasta made from buckwheat.

Togarashi: Japanese dried and ground red chile.

Yuzu: A citrus fruit with a wonderfully tropical lemon-lime–Mandarin orange taste. You can buy it as a fresh fruit or as bottled juice.

OSHITASHI *Serves 4*

2 large bunches fresh spinach

3 cups chilled Dashi Broth (page 136)

¼ cup mirin rice wine

¼ cup sake

2 tablespoons soy sauce (preferably Japanese shoyu soy sauce)

4 pinches of bonito flakes

8 shiso leaves, stacked, rolled lengthwise, and sliced crosswise into thin ribbons

Mitsuba or fresh chervil leaves, finely chopped (optional)

Myoga ginger buds, thinly sliced crosswise (optional)

Soy Sauce, Shoyu, and Tamari

When a recipe calls for soy sauce, what do you buy? I prefer the Japanese rendition of soy sauce, which is called shoyu. It is a little sweeter and richer than Chinese soy sauce but also has a lighter, less salty flavor. If you can't eat wheat or are gluten sensitive, try tamari, a wheat-free version.

You'll see a lot of Japanese influences in my recipes as well as in my design. Oshitashi, a chilled spinach dish, is still one of my ultimate comfort foods. It's made of spinach quickly blanched in boiling water, chilled, drained, and compressed into a tight cylinder, then sliced and served with salty/savory chilled dashi. I like to sprinkle a little fresh shiso leaf over the top—shiso is really easy to grow as an herb, kind of like parsley or cilantro.

1 Fill a large bowl with ice and cold water. Bring a large saucepan of salted water to a boil. Add about half of the spinach, making sure to submerge all of the leaves. Once it wilts, after 15 to 20 seconds, use a slotted spoon or frying spider to transfer it to the ice water. Repeat with the remaining spinach.

2 Drain the spinach in a sieve and use a rubber spatula to press out as much liquid from the leaves as possible. Place half of the spinach on a doubled square of paper towel and wrap the spinach in the towel, then squeeze it into a cylinder that is roughly 6" long. Unwrap it; it should be formed into a very compact cylinder that holds together. Repeat with the remaining spinach, then slice each cylinder crosswise into six equal pieces. Place three spinach bundles on each plate.

3 Stir together the dashi, mirin, sake, and soy sauce in a 4-cup liquid measuring cup. Divide the sauce over the spinach. Finish each serving with a pinch of bonito, shiso ribbons, mitsuba (if using), and myoga (if using).

RAW CORN, TOMATO, AND COUSCOUS SALAD

Serves 4

1 teaspoon kosher salt

½ cup couscous

2 ears corn, husked

1 pound ripe tomatoes, cored and chopped

½ cup fresh basil leaves, stacked, rolled lengthwise, and sliced crosswise into thin ribbons

2 tablespoons finely chopped fresh chives

Juice of ½ lemon

1 tablespoon extra-virgin olive oil

½ teaspoon freshly ground black pepper

Did you know how easy it is to make couscous? You simply add it to boiling water, wait a few minutes, and—like magic—it's done! Here I use ultrafresh ingredients from local farms to make a couscous salad that is my kind of late summertime fast food. Using local produce feels so good. It's also worthwhile to seek out and support farmers who are committed to growing beautiful produce without harmful chemicals.

1 Add 1 cup of water to a small saucepan. Add ½ teaspoon of the salt and bring the water to a boil over high heat. Add the couscous, return the liquid to a boil, turn off the heat, and immediately cover the saucepan. Set the couscous aside while you make the salad.

2 Slice the tip off of an ear of corn and hold the ear by the nub of the cob at the end. Slice down from top to bottom to remove a strip of corn kernels, then lay the cob on the flat side and slice away the kernels from the other three sides of the cob. Repeat with the other ear and transfer the corn kernels to a large bowl.

3 Add the tomatoes, basil, chives, lemon juice, olive oil, remaining ½ teaspoon of salt, and the pepper. Uncover the couscous and fluff it with a fork, then add it to the corn mixture. Stir to combine and taste to see if the salad needs more salt, pepper, lemon juice, or olive oil. Serve at room temperature or cold.

FLOWERS: PLANNING AND ARRANGING

A few years ago, I decided to restore a garden bed that had been neglected for years. It has three tiers that rise up a slight hillside, and I can easily imagine that it was once a vibrant flower garden, though it was now overgrown with weeds and grasses. I cleared it out, created allées, and went a little crazy purchasing new varieties of perennial flowering plants. Every year I look forward to spring to see how it flourishes and fills in. Each spring I add to its abundance by picking new blooms and annuals to make that year's garden unique and special. Clipping stems and gathering flowers to make a gorgeous bouquet from my own garden is one of my most precious joys in the summer and early fall.

1 small tomato, cored, seeded, and chopped

1 scallion, very thinly sliced on a bias

½ cup finely chopped mango

½ small cucumber, peeled (if the skin is tough), seeded, and chopped

½ medium orange, red, or yellow bell pepper, finely chopped

¼ medium Vidalia onion, finely chopped

1½ tablespoons finely chopped fresh cilantro leaves

½ teaspoon finely chopped fresh tarragon or fennel fronds (optional)

1 cup shelled lump crab meat, picked through for shells (from about 1 pound of crab)

Juice of ½ lime

1½ teaspoons distilled white vinegar

1 teaspoon curry powder (optional)

¾ teaspoon Dijon mustard

¼ teaspoon fine sea salt

¼ teaspoon freshly ground black pepper

1 tablespoon extra-virgin olive oil

1 small avocado, halved, pitted, peeled, and finely chopped

Cored and seeded tomato halves, large Bibb lettuce leaves, or toast, for serving

STONE CRAB SALAD *Serves 4*

I created this salad on a Bahama island that takes several modes of transport to get to and has lots of little pink houses and stunning pink sand beaches. I jumped in the ocean, and then my guests and I found ourselves famished. Instead of choosing standard resort food, I went to the local fishing boat, bought some fresh crab claws, and found the rest of the ingredients for this delicious salad in a local market. It was refreshing and satisfying, too, plus since the crab claws were already steamed (or you can just buy lump crab meat at the store), no cooking was needed. It all comes together superfast, making it fairly vacation-perfect.

1 Add the chopped tomato, scallion, mango, cucumber, bell pepper, onion, cilantro, tarragon (if using), and crab meat to a medium bowl and toss gently to combine.

2 Whisk together the lime juice, vinegar, curry powder (if using), mustard, salt, and black pepper in a small bowl. While whisking, slowly drizzle in the olive oil until the vinaigrette is creamy and well emulsified.

3 Pour the vinaigrette over the crab salad and gently toss to combine. Add the avocado and stir once so as not to smash the delicate pieces. Serve in a tomato half, on lettuce leaves, or on a piece of toast.

GRILLED SQUID SALAD

Serves 4

Squid and Salad
1 pound whole squid
(or squid rings)

1 tablespoon extra-
virgin olive oil

1 teaspoon finely
chopped fresh thyme
leaves or ½ teaspoon
dried

½ teaspoon dried
oregano

½ teaspoon sea salt

½ teaspoon freshly
ground black pepper

¼ teaspoon onion
powder

Pinch of red-pepper
flakes

6 cups arugula

1 ripe tomato, halved
and thinly sliced

Rice Vinegar Dressing
3 tablespoons rice
vinegar

1 tablespoon fresh
lemon juice

1 teaspoon soy sauce,
plus more to taste if
needed

Pinch of sea salt

2 tablespoons extra-
virgin olive oil

I love to shop in local markets when I travel, especially if I have
a kitchen to use wherever I am staying. You learn so much
about other cultures and people when you buy fish from a local
fisherman or stop at a farm stand off the side of a road. This
salad is exactly the kind of simple, flavorful, light meal I like to
make. I often make it when I'm in the Bahamas, where I am
practically guaranteed to find great fresh fish and produce. I
love how the edges and tendrils of the squid get charred and
crisp over an open flame—it really brings a wonderfully complex flavor to the otherwise very simple salad. And you don't
have to worry about it sticking to the grill grates either—squid
is a pretty low-anxiety seafood to prepare.

---

1 *To make the squid:* Toss the squid with the olive oil, thyme,
oregano, salt, black pepper, onion powder, and red-pepper
flakes in a large bowl and set aside. Set a charcoal or gas grill to
high heat (meaning you can hold your hand 4" above the grill
grate for 1 to 2 seconds before it feels too hot). Place the squid
on the grill and cook until they char and turn opaque, turning
them midway through cooking, 2 to 3 minutes total (if using
squid rings, grill them in a grill basket so the rings don't fall
through the grill grates). Remove the squid from the grill and
transfer to a cutting board to cool slightly before slicing the
bodies crosswise into rings (keep the tentacles intact).

2 *To make the dressing:* Whisk the vinegar, lemon juice, soy
sauce, and salt together in a small bowl. While whisking, slowly
drizzle in the olive oil until the dressing is thick and creamy,
about 1 minute. Taste and add more soy sauce, if needed.

3 *To make the salad:* Arrange the arugula over a large platter
and arrange the tomato slices over the arugula. Turn the squid
out over the greens and drizzle the dressing over the squid.
Serve immediately.

CHILLED CORN BISQUE

Serves 4

5 large ears corn, husked

4 cups store-bought or homemade chicken broth (page 208)

2 dried bay leaves

1 teaspoon whole coriander seeds

1 teaspoon whole fennel seeds

1 teaspoon freshly ground black pepper

¼ teaspoon sumac (optional)

1 tablespoon unsalted butter

1 medium yellow onion, finely chopped

1 leek, white and light green parts only, thinly sliced

3 medium garlic cloves, minced

¾ teaspoon fine sea salt

½ cup half-and-half

4 large mint leaves, stacked, rolled lengthwise, and sliced crosswise into thin ribbons

Edible-quality marigold flower petals (optional)

When I'm out at the country house and the corn hits the farm stands in the summertime, I'm all over it! To preserve its sweet goodness, I love using corn raw like in a salad such as Raw Corn, Tomato, and Couscous Salad (page 85) or cooking it only very slightly to encourage the starches to soften and natural sweetness to intensify. You can dress this soup up by topping it with a mound of lump crab meat, some poached and chilled shrimp, steamed lobster, or even chunks of avocado. A little sprinkle of edible flowers gives the soup the most delicate appearance; I like using marigold petals to echo the golden hue of the soup.

1 Slice the tip off of an ear of corn and hold the ear by the nub of the cob at the end. Slice down from top to bottom to remove a strip of corn kernels, then lay the cob on the flat side and slice away the kernels from the other three sides of the cob. Repeat with the other ears (you should end up with about 5 cups of corn). Place the corn kernels in a medium bowl and transfer the cobs to a large pot.

2 Make the corn stock: Add the chicken broth, bay leaves, coriander, fennel, pepper, and sumac (if using) to the pot with the corncobs. Bring the broth to a boil over high heat, reduce the heat to medium-low, and gently simmer for 10 minutes. Turn off the heat and set the pot aside to allow the corncobs to infuse the stock.

3 Meanwhile, sauté the corn: Melt the butter in a large skillet over medium-high heat. Add the onion, leek, garlic, and salt, reduce the heat to medium-low, and cook, stirring often, until the onion is soft and translucent, about 5 minutes. Stir in the corn and continue to cook, stirring often, until the kernels become bright yellow and taste sweet and juicy, about 2 minutes.

recipe continues

4 Strain the corn stock through a fine-mesh sieve into a medium bowl. Add three-quarters of the sautéed corn and onion mixture to a blender, add the corn stock, and blend until very smooth, 1 to 2 minutes. Add the half-and-half and blend until well combined, about 30 seconds. Taste and add more salt or half-and-half (for a thinner consistency) if needed. Refrigerate the soup until it is chilled (or serve at room temperature).

5 Divide the soup among bowls. Sprinkle with the remaining corn mixture, the mint, and marigold petals (if using) and serve.

Savory Whipped Cream

A little dollop of savory whipped cream on top of chilled soup is an unexpected and creative embellishment that adds a note of pure decadence. Pour ¾ cup of cream into a large bowl and whip it by hand (or use a hand mixer or a stand mixer) until it holds medium-stiff peaks. Then add your savory embellishment—like freshly ground black pepper, ground sumac, turmeric powder, curry powder, finely chopped fresh herbs . . . you get the idea! Spoon some cream onto the soup and serve immediately.

SPICY POBLANO SOUP

Serves 4 to 6

6 poblano chile peppers

1 tablespoon extra-virgin olive oil

3 cups store-bought or homemade chicken broth (page 208)

1 large russet potato (I like to leave the peel on), roughly chopped

½ teaspoon ground nutmeg

1 teaspoon fine sea salt, plus more to taste

¼ teaspoon freshly ground black pepper

3 tablespoons melted butter

1 tablespoon all-purpose flour

2 cups whole milk, warmed

Finely chopped fresh cilantro, for serving

¼ cup sour cream, for serving

I was in my local market in New York City food shopping for a weekend in the country, and I saw this spotlight of deep green calling to me: shiny, twisty poblano peppers. They reminded me of a trip I took to Mexico City, and I tried to re-create the flavors of that trip—smoke, heat, earthy spice, and comfort—in this soup. I highly recommend grilling the poblanos instead of broiling—the smoky flavor is a complete game changer.

1 Adjust the oven rack to the highest position and heat the broiler to high (or heat a charcoal or gas grill to high if grilling the chiles). Place the chiles on a rimmed sheet pan, toss with the olive oil, and broil until charred on all sides, turning them often, about 15 minutes.

2 Place the chiles in a paper bag or in a bowl and cover with plastic wrap. Set them aside for 15 minutes to steam and cool, then peel away the charred skin. Remove the stems and seeds and set the chiles aside (wash your hands well after handling chiles; don't rub your eyes; and never place chiles under water to help you remove the skin—it robs the flavor).

3 While the chiles roast and cool, bring the chicken broth to a simmer in a medium saucepan over medium-high heat. Add the potato and cook until it easily mashes against the side of the pan, 16 to 22 minutes. Set aside to cool slightly.

4 Add the chiles, chicken broth and potato mixture, nutmeg, salt, and black pepper to a blender and purée until smooth.

5 Melt the butter in a medium saucepan over medium-high heat. Reduce the heat to medium-low and whisk in the flour, making sure to stir out any lumps. Add the warm milk a little at a time, stirring well between additions, to create a smooth base.

6 Increase the heat to medium and stir in the pepper–chicken broth mixture. Continue to cook until the flavors come together, tasting and adjusting the salt and pepper if needed. Divide among bowls and serve with cilantro and a dollop of sour cream.

QUICK WHOLE BRANZINO WITH LIME AND LEMONGRASS *Serves 2 to 4*

1 whole branzino (1½ pounds) or other flaky fish such as snapper or sea bass, cleaned

1½ teaspoons coarse sea salt

1 teaspoon freshly ground black pepper

1 lime, ½ of it thinly sliced

3 tablespoons extra-virgin olive oil

2 large sprigs fresh thyme

3 large sprigs fresh herb of choice (such as basil, chervil, dill, parsley, rosemary, tarragon)

1 stalk lemongrass, outer layer removed, inner reed sliced in half lengthwise and smashed with a knife

People always ask me, when do I find the time to cook. My life is nonstop—it seems like I'm always toggling between being on set for *Project Runway*, designing a new collection, or doing press; needless to say, my work days often blur well into the night. When I leave the atelier or a long meeting and walk into the New York night, I realize, quite suddenly, that I am completely starving! My solution is often to make it to the fish market before it closes to grab a whole branzino. It might sound fancy or elaborate, but really, cooking branzino takes just 20 minutes. It also makes a great main course for company, and in that case, I'll roast two!

1 Adjust an oven rack to the upper-middle position and heat the broiler to high. Line a 13" x 9" baking dish with aluminum foil.

2 Set the fish on a cutting board and pat it dry. Use a sharp knife to make 2"-long slits across each side of the fish, spacing them about 1½" apart. Combine the salt and pepper in a small bowl, then liberally season both sides and the inside of the fish. Place the fish in the prepared baking dish.

3 Squeeze the lime half over both sides of the fish, then rub both sides and the inside with the olive oil. Place half of the lime slices in the fish, tuck the herb sprigs between the lemongrass halves, and then place the bundle on top of the lime slices. Cover the herb bundle with the remaining lime slices.

4 Broil until the skin is browned and crisp, about 8 minutes (watch the fish closely as broiler intensities vary). Carefully turn the fish to the other side. Broil the other side until crisp and browned, another 6 to 8 minutes or so.

5 Remove the fish from the oven and poke a knife into one of the slits. The fish should be opaque down to the bone (it will be juicy from the olive oil and lime juice) and flake easily. Remove it from the oven, transfer to a platter, and serve immediately.

LINGUINE CON LE VONGOLE *Serves 6*

Soaking Clams

Make sure to soak the clams for at least 20 minutes to allow them to expel any sand trapped inside. If the clams are especially sandy on the outside, let them soak for 30 minutes, then clean out the bowl and refill with fresh water and ice and soak for an additional 30 minutes before using. Few things are more disappointing than taking a bite of a gorgeous linguine con le vongole and having it be marred by grit.

The year I was working on my first collection, when I was 21 years old, I found a mentor in Kal Ruttenstein, the illustrious fashion director at Bloomingdale's in New York. Kal was a huge source of encouragement, and it was through him that I found a deeply personal connection to American fashion. Kal was also a bit of a gourmand; he'd invite me to dinner and we'd talk about the theater, American fashion, trends, and, of course, what we should have for dessert. After I finished my first collection, the iconic editor of Italian *Vogue*, Franca Sozzani, invited me to Italy during Milan's fashion week to visit the great Italian fabric mills as part of a special award I won in an international design competition. Kal happened to be in Milan as well, and he invited me to Da Giacomo, a restaurant world-famous for its fish, old-world décor, and energetic buzz.

We sat at a center table, and as the first course of linguine con le vongole (clams) arrived, I began to feel as if all eyes were on me. Buyers, fashion editors, journalists—they all came to talk to Kal and compare notes, talk about fashion week, and, of course, gossip. I had no idea who they were but could sense they were important. Only after the panna cotta was devoured and the espresso drunk did Kal tell me who they all were: Yves Carcelles, the president of LVMH (Louis Vuitton, Fendi, Céline); Sidney Toledano, the CEO of Christian Dior; and Domenico DeSole, the CEO of Gucci. All in one evening, all in one blurred frenzy of food and wine and words. It was an evening that I will certainly never forget! It often strikes me how noteworthy memories are often affixed to taste memories—for me, that evening will forever be linked to linguine con le vongole.

The dish is now a staple at my house, because it's delicious and I can whip it up for friends or myself in just 20 minutes (really!). Stella Madrid Schnabel, a close friend of mine, will often engage me in heated debates about what you can and can't add to linguine con le vongole. We both agree that cherry or

recipe continues

grape tomatoes, halved and tossed in with the pasta, are a perfectly acceptable addition.

4 tablespoons coarse sea salt, plus a few pinches for seasoning

3 pounds cherrystone, littleneck, or manila clams (manila clams are smaller and generally tend to be sweeter than cherrystones or littlenecks)

1 pound linguine

2 tablespoons extra-virgin olive oil

4 medium garlic cloves, finely chopped

Red-pepper flakes

½ cup fresh flat-leaf parsley leaves, finely chopped

1¼ cups dry white wine

Freshly ground black pepper

1 Add a little hot water to a large bowl and stir in 1 tablespoon of the salt until it dissolves. Fill the bowl with cold water and ice, then add the clams and set aside for at least 20 minutes or longer. Transfer the clams to a colander and scrub them under cold running water to remove any remaining sand and grit.

2 Set a large pot of water over high heat. Add 3 tablespoons of the salt (you want the pasta water to taste like sea water) and bring the water to a boil. Add the linguine and boil until it's cooked about halfway (it will still be solid white in the middle), about 6 minutes. Drain the linguine.

3 While the pasta cooks, start the sauce: Add the olive oil and garlic to a large, deep skillet over medium heat. Cook the garlic, stirring often, until it just becomes fragrant, 1 to 2 minutes (you don't want the garlic to brown). Add a few pinches of red-pepper flakes and the clams and cook, stirring occasionally, for 2 minutes, then add half of the parsley. Cover the skillet and cook, shaking the pan occasionally, for 2 minutes (you want the clams to just start opening before you add the wine).

4 Uncover the pan, add the wine, re-cover the pan, and steam the clams until they open, about 5 minutes. Add the linguine to the pan, reduce the heat to low, and vigorously toss the linguine with the clams and wine sauce. The starch from the pasta will work into the sauce, and the clam juices and wine will help to finish cooking the pasta. Continue to stir and toss for 2 minutes, then season the pasta with a few pinches of salt and the remaining parsley. Continue to stir and toss the pasta in the sauce over heat until the pasta is perfectly al dente and the sauce is thick and clings to the pasta (and isn't watery), 1 to 2 minutes longer. Taste and adjust the seasoning with more salt if needed and black pepper.

RESTAURANT PASTA AT HOME

You go to a restaurant and order a bowl of pasta. How is it always so silky and rich and wonderful? The secret is in two techniques that are *so easy* for all home cooks to start using: Adding pasta cooking water to your sauce is trick one, and finishing the cooking of your pasta in the actual sauce is trick two.

"Trick one and trick two."

You know the cooking water that you boil your pasta in? That stuff is cooking gold! Not only is it seasoned (you know how you always boil pasta in water that should taste pleasantly of sea water), but it is full of starch that the pasta releases as it boils. Add a little of that (about ½ cup) to your sauce—from pesto to garlic and oil or even Bolognese—and the cooking water adds a silky quality and also helps the sauce "stick" to the pasta.

The second trick is to actually finish the pasta in the sauce you're serving it with. Why? Because the pasta will absorb some of the sauce, thereby flavoring it, *and* it will also thicken the sauce from the starches it releases as it finishes its last minute or two in the sauce. Just keep shaking the pan and tossing the pasta occasionally to encourage even cooking.

PASTA PUTTANESCA *Serves 4*

1 pound spaghetti

1 tablespoon plus
½ teaspoon sea salt

2 tablespoons extra-virgin olive oil

3 medium garlic cloves, roughly chopped

6 anchovies, plus
1 teaspoon of oil from the tin

2 tablespoons miso paste (preferably red miso)

2 tablespoons tomato paste

1 can (28 ounces) whole peeled tomatoes, shredded by hand

10 large basil leaves, roughly torn

½ teaspoon freshly ground black pepper

¾ cup pitted kalamata olives, halved

1 tablespoon brine-packed capers

Imagine Saraghina, the lusty harlot from Federico Fellini's 1963 film, *8½*, dancing on the beach. This to me is reminiscent of pasta puttanesca, which literally translates as the pasta sauce of the prostitute. Why is it called this? Because the sauce is bold—it's briny and salty and spicy! For even more sultriness, I mix some miso paste into the tomato paste. The miso brings a wonderfully savory, fermented depth that makes the sauce even more fantastic. Red miso is a little deeper and funkier tasting than white, and that's the kind I prefer in this sauce, but really any kind of miso will work.

1 Bring a large pot of water to a boil. Add the pasta and 1 tablespoon of the salt and cook until al dente. Set aside ½ cup of pasta water, then drain the pasta and set aside.

2 Add the olive oil and garlic to a large skillet and set it over medium-high heat. Once the garlic becomes fragrant, after about 30 seconds, add the anchovies and anchovy oil. Reduce the heat to medium and use a fork to mash the anchovies into the hot oil and garlic. Continue to cook, stirring often, until the mixture looks pasty, about 2 minutes.

3 While the pasta cooks, make the sauce: Stir the miso and tomato paste together in a small bowl, then add it to the garlic-anchovy mixture. Cook until it begins to break down, about 3 minutes, then add the tomatoes, basil, the remaining ½ teaspoon of salt, and the pepper and simmer, stirring occasionally, until you see some oil collect at the surface, about 10 minutes. Add the reserved pasta water a splash at a time to make the sauce looser, if needed.

4 Stir in the olives and capers, taste, and add more salt if needed. Add the spaghetti to the skillet and toss to combine. Divide among four pasta bowls and serve.

SUMMER CORN FETTUCCINE WITH ZUCCHINI AND BURRATA *Serves 4*

2 ears corn, husked

1 tablespoon plus
1 teaspoon fine sea salt

1 medium zucchini,
ends removed,
zucchini sliced
lengthwise into thin
planks, then stacked
and sliced lengthwise
into thin strips (or
use a spiralizer to turn
the zucchini into
"zoodles" or buy
8 ounces of precut
"zoodles")

1 pound fettuccine

2 tablespoons
unsalted butter

2 teaspoons extra-
virgin olive oil

3 garlic cloves,
smashed and peeled

¼ cup heavy cream

1 cup fresh basil
leaves, stacked, rolled
lengthwise, and sliced
crosswise into thin
ribbons

1 ball (8 ounces)
burrata cheese

2 zucchini flowers,
thinly sliced
crosswise (optional)

I think my commitment to fresh ingredients comes from my deep love of the natural world. To look at the complexity of a flower—be it a bearded iris or a zucchini blossom—and examine how it is constructed absolutely inspires how I design my dresses and gowns. To see a zucchini developing on the vine and to know the right moment to pick it is thrilling to me. There is absolutely nothing better than harvesting fresh vegetables from the garden and knowing that what you're preparing to put into your body was growing in the garden just moments ago. This recipe is my idea of the perfect late summer pasta: sweet corn, sweet zucchini, and silky-soft (and yes, sinful!) burrata cheese.

1 Slice the tip off of an ear of corn and hold the ear by the nub of the cob at the end. Slice down from top to bottom to remove a strip of corn kernels, then lay the cob on the flat side and slice away the kernels from the other three sides of the cob. Repeat with the other ear and add the corn kernels to a large bowl. Set aside. Place the cobs in a large pot of water along with 1 tablespoon of the salt. Bring the water to a boil over high heat. Reduce the heat to medium and simmer the corncobs for 15 minutes.

2 Meanwhile, fill a medium bowl with ice and cold water and set aside. Bring a medium pot of water to a boil. Add the remaining 1 teaspoon of salt and the zucchini and cook just until the zucchini becomes limp, 1 to 2 minutes. Drain in a colander or fine-mesh sieve and plunge the zucchini into the ice water to stop the cooking process; once the zucchini is cool, drain and set aside.

recipe continues

3 Add the pasta to the water with the corncobs and cook following the package instructions until it is just a little shy of being al dente (the pasta will finish cooking in the sauce). Use a ladle to set aside ¼ cup of cooking water. Drain the pasta in a colander and remove and discard the corncobs.

4 Add the butter and olive oil to a large skillet. Heat over medium heat until the butter starts to melt, then add the garlic and cook, stirring occasionally, until the garlic is fragrant, 1 to 2 minutes. Add the corn and cook until it turns bright yellow, 30 seconds. Add the cream, pasta water, and pasta and cook, stirring and shaking the pan often and using tongs to toss the pasta in the sauce, until the sauce thickens and the pasta is perfectly al dente, 1 to 2 minutes.

5 Turn off the heat and quickly toss in the zucchini and three-quarters of the basil. Divide the pasta among four pasta bowls. Place the burrata on a plate and cut into quarters. Top each serving with a piece of the burrata (and any cream that pooled on the plate), sprinkle with the remaining basil and zucchini flowers (if using), and serve.

FARMING ON THE ROOF

There is no question that the fresher the produce, the better the results. While the rooftop garden idea may seem like a millennial innovation, we actually had one on the roof of our SoHo building when I was a young boy, and going up there with my mother to plant seedlings and harvest vegetables marks the beginning of my horticultural education.

My mom and I planted two of everything in the rooftop raised beds—it was like an edible Noah's Ark! We had cherry tomatoes, Concord grapes, pickling cucumbers, and even small cantaloupes and strawberries (that rarely survived the trip down to the loft—we'd gobble them up on the spot!). Growing things on the roof was no easy task; we had to water every day to keep parched plants happy in the sweltering late summer heat, which, in New York's asphalt jungle, lasts well into September and even to mid-October. I even had "roof friends"—neighbors on adjoining roofs who rejoiced in their own abundant gardens in the sky and who shared their rooftop gardening wisdom with me.

The rooftop functioned as a kind of backyard for a city kid like me without a traditional house and yard. The garden was fun but really didn't produce enough to satisfy our needs, so we'd supplement with weekly trips to the green market in Union Square, where we'd add to our bounty with produce grown in farms surrounding the NYC area.

A BAHAMIAN LOVE AFFAIR

Besides the fact that it's gorgeous and drenched in sunshine, another reason why I choose the Bahamas to escape to for a quick mini-vacation is its food. In the Bahamas you can find the most buttery avocados, several varieties of perfectly sweet-ripe and just-picked mangoes, island spices, and wonderful produce that comes in all colors of the rainbow.

Of course, tourists and cruise ships can overcrowd some islands, but if you do your homework and find the right island, you can luck out with a peaceful retreat. Plus, I really love the way Bahamians cook with spices and strong curry flavors, so I'm eager to find a quiet spot in exchange for the promise of a great culinary experience. There will usually be a fisherman near a dock from whom you can buy some lobster or grouper, and there's probably a farm stand nearby, too, where you can purchase peppery arugula, herbs, bell peppers, lemongrass, and other island treats. I even once made sea grape jelly on a vacation there, though it turned out just like really intense Concord grape jelly!

1 tablespoon extra-virgin olive oil

3 tablespoons unsalted butter or ghee

1 piece (3" long) fresh gingerroot, peeled, thinly sliced, stacked, and sliced lengthwise into matchsticks

2 medium garlic cloves, smashed and roughly chopped

½ large white onion, finely chopped

1 teaspoon fine sea salt

2 tablespoons curry powder

1 tablespoon ground turmeric (or 2 small knobs fresh turmeric, peeled and thinly sliced)

3 strips lime peel

1 stalk lemongrass, tough outer layer removed, stalk halved lengthwise and sliced crosswise on an angle into 2" pieces

½–1 spicy chile pepper (such as a Thai bird's eye chile or a Scotch bonnet or habanero), finely chopped (seeded for less heat)

4 small tomatoes, quartered

1 can (13½ ounces) coconut milk

1 orange bell pepper, seeded and finely chopped

ingredients continue

CARIBBEAN LOBSTER TAILS WITH COCONUT CURRY

Serves 4

I was inspired to make this Bahamian curry from watching the local women on Harbour Island in the Caribbean, who are just the most amazing cooks. Chiles, coconut, lemongrass, ginger, herbs . . . they all contribute to the lusciousness and exceptionally fragrant beauty of this curry that is so ideal with lobster tails. I try to keep a few lobster tails in my freezer specifically to make this dish. It's so elegant looking and really very simple to make for company. I like to stuff the tails with aromatics and run them under the broiler for a few minutes, then finish the tails in the curry. For company I'll remove the tail meat from the shells and then place the meat back in the shell so no one has to struggle with removing the lobster meat at the table. You can also substitute cleaned and shelled shrimp or monkfish (plan on about ¼ pound per person) instead of lobster tails—add the shrimp or monkfish (people often refer to it as poor man's lobster) to the curry with the coconut milk in step 2, cover, and gently cook until opaque and tender, 3 to 5 minutes.

1 Heat the olive oil and 1 tablespoon of the butter in a large pot over medium-high heat. Once the butter is melted, add the ginger and garlic and cook, stirring often, until fragrant, about 30 seconds. Reduce the heat to medium and stir in the onion and salt. Continue cooking until they become soft, stirring often, about 2 minutes. Stir in the curry powder and turmeric and reduce the heat to medium-low.

2 Stir in the lime peel, lemongrass, and chile pepper. Once the lime is fragrant, after about 2 minutes, increase the heat to medium and stir in the tomatoes. Cook, stirring often, until

recipe continues

1 cup store-bought or homemade chicken broth (page 208) or vegetable broth

1 sprig fresh thyme

1 makrut lime leaf (optional)

4 lobster tails (defrosted under cool running water for 20 minutes if frozen)

12 large fresh basil leaves, plus ½ cup fresh basil leaves, stacked, rolled lengthwise, and sliced crosswise into thin ribbons

½ lemon, thinly sliced

Freshly ground black pepper

1 tablespoon honey

1 lime, cut into wedges

the tomatoes begin to soften, 5 to 8 minutes. Then pour in the coconut milk and increase the heat to medium-high to bring the coconut milk to a simmer. Reduce the heat to medium-low and cook until the sauce is slightly thick, about 5 minutes.

3 Stir in half of the bell pepper, the broth, thyme, and lime leaf (if using) and simmer gently for 20 minutes, stirring occasionally. Turn off the heat.

4 Adjust the oven rack to the upper-middle position and heat the broiler to high. Line a baking dish with aluminum foil. Set the lobster tails on a cutting board flat belly side facing up and use kitchen shears to make a slit from one end to the other straight through the shell (take care not to cut into the meat). Squeeze open the tail to expose the flesh and remove any shell fragments you see. Stuff each tail with three basil leaves and a piece of lemon followed by ½ tablespoon of butter and a pinch of black pepper.

5 Set the lobster tails in the foil-lined baking dish and broil until the meat is opaque around the edges but still pink-pearlescent in the center, 2 to 3½ minutes (you cannot walk away; otherwise, you could burn the tails!). Remove the baking dish from the broiler, cover the tails with a sheet of foil, and let them rest for 10 minutes.

6 Meanwhile, strain the sauce through a fine-mesh sieve and return it to a clean pot or deep skillet. Return the sauce to a simmer over medium heat and stir in the honey. Place the lobster tails cut side down in the sauce and warm them up there for 1 minute. Turn off the heat. Remove the lobster tails from the sauce, remove and discard the lemon slices and basil leaves, and use a knife to separate the meat from the tail in each one (so your guests can get at the meat more easily). Use a spoon to add a good amount of sauce to four bowls. Place a broiled tail in the center of each bowl, cut side up, and sprinkle with the remaining bell pepper and some sliced basil. Serve with a lime wedge.

LOCAL FISH FILLETS WITH FRIED MEYER LEMON AND MINT *Serves 4*

1 pound skin-on ¼"- to ½"-thick fish fillets (such as fluke, red snapper, trout, grouper, striped bass, or flounder), cut crosswise into 4 equal pieces

1 teaspoon kosher salt

½ teaspoon freshly ground black pepper

1 tablespoon unsalted butter

1 tablespoon extra-virgin olive oil

¼ cup fresh mint leaves

2 Meyer lemons, ends removed and the lemons sliced into ¼"-thick rounds

My favorite nearby escape from New York City is the Hamptons, especially when it is off-season. I enjoy the beautiful stretch of largely deserted beach and, usually through November, wonderfully gorgeous weather. I'm always in the mood for a breezy, healthy meal when I'm at the beach. Being so close to the ocean, I find that it makes the most sense to buy fish that is fresh and local, and since this technique works with any fillet, you should feel a sense of freedom when buying the fish, be it from a fisherman or market. After turning the fish, I sometimes like to add capers or chopped pitted green olives, too.

1 Blot the fish fillets dry, then season with the salt and pepper. Use a sharp knife to make two shallow diagonal slashes through the skin of each fillet (this prevents it from curling).

2 Add the butter and olive oil to a large nonstick skillet over medium-high heat and swirl until the butter is melted. Add the mint leaves to the pan, then place the lemon slices in two rows in the skillet. Lay each fillet, flesh side down, over one row of lemon rounds and cook until the lemon is browned and the edges of the fish become opaque and feel firm, about 4 minutes for ¼" fillets and 6 minutes for ½" fillets.

3 Use a fish spatula to carefully turn the fillets over, trying to capture the lemon slices and mint as well. Cook until the skin is crisp and browned, 3 to 4 minutes.

4 Slide the fillets out onto a platter and cover with the mint and any sauce in the pan. Serve immediately.

POACHED SALMON
WITH LIME TZATZIKI

Serves 4

Poached Salmon

2 cups dry white wine

6 sprigs fresh thyme

1 small carrot, quartered crosswise

1 small rib celery, quartered crosswise

1 lemon, thinly sliced into wheels

¼ medium yellow onion, quartered

1 teaspoon fine sea salt

2 sprigs fresh dill

1½ pounds fresh salmon fillets, pin bones removed

Lime Tzatziki

1 cup sour cream

½ cup full-fat or reduced-fat plain Greek yogurt

½ medium cucumber, peeled and grated on the large-hole side of a box grater

Juice of 1 lime

2 tablespoons finely chopped fresh flat-leaf parsley

½ teaspoon fine sea salt

Fresh, light, and so pretty (not to mention loaded with omega-3s for healthy, shiny hair and glowing skin!), salmon is a quick and delicious weekday dinner. Poaching is even simpler than broiling or roasting—it takes less than 10 minutes, and, if you're sensitive to the smell of cooking fish, poaching is a great fragrance-free method. Wild salmon is usually thinner than farmed salmon and will poach more quickly, so keep that in mind when you start your poaching time. Sometimes I'll make some quick Cucumber-Turmeric Pickles (page 15) to serve alongside for a bright flavor with some crunch.

1 *To make the poached salmon:* Pour the white wine and 1 cup of water into a large, deep skillet. Add the thyme, carrot, celery, lemon, onion, and salt and bring to a boil. Add the dill, then slide the fish, skin side down, into the pan and return to a simmer.

2 Reduce the heat to low and cover the pan. Gently poach for 5 minutes. Turn off the heat and set aside until the center of the fish resists light pressure and the fish is firm at the edges, 5 to 8 minutes depending on the thickness of the fillet.

3 *To make the lime tzatziki:* Stir the sour cream, yogurt, cucumber, lime juice, parsley, and salt together in a medium bowl. Taste and adjust with more salt if needed.

4 Use a flat spatula to lift the fish from the pan. Place a paper towel beneath it and quickly blot it dry, then transfer the fish to a platter. Dollop the tzatziki over the fish and serve.

COMFORTING CHICKEN CURRY *Serves 4*

1½ pounds boneless chicken thighs, chopped into bite-size pieces

1½ teaspoons garam masala

1½ teaspoons fine sea salt

½ teaspoon freshly ground black pepper

1 tablespoon ghee or unsalted butter

1 whole garlic clove, peeled

1 makrut lime leaf or 2 long strips lime peel (remove any white pith)

1 piece (1" long) gingerroot, peeled and thinly sliced into matchsticks

1 medium red onion, finely chopped

1 tablespoon curry powder

1 tablespoon tomato paste

2 plum tomatoes, cored and chopped

1 medium red bell pepper, halved, seeded, and thinly sliced

1 medium yellow bell pepper, halved, seeded, and thinly sliced

½ cup store-bought or homemade chicken broth (page 208)

This chicken curry showcases many curry flavors that I've experienced through my travels. Curry can encompass a wide range of flavors and spice levels (see the box on the next page); here I combine some of my favorite curry influences like makrut lime leaves, garam masala, fresh vegetables, coconut milk, and basil to make a curry that delights me. I love this over quick sautéed boneless chicken thighs, which are juicier and more flavorful and tender than boneless breast meat (but really either can be used). You *must* serve this with lots of steamed white rice (preferably fluffy jasmine rice).

1 Place the chicken in a large bowl and add the garam masala, salt, and black pepper. Use your hands to work the spices onto all sides of the chicken pieces.

2 Add the ghee and garlic to a large skillet over medium-low heat. Slowly cook the garlic, turning the clove often, until it becomes golden, 4 to 5 minutes. Increase the heat to medium-high and add the chicken pieces to the pan. Cook, stirring occasionally, until they begin to brown on all sides, about 6 minutes (if the garlic starts to turn too brown, remove it from the pan).

3 Stir in the makrut lime leaf and ginger and cook, stirring often, until the ginger is fragrant, about 2 minutes. Stir in the onion and cook, stirring often, until it starts to soften, about 2 minutes, then add the curry powder and tomato paste and stir to coat the chicken pieces. Add the tomatoes and bell peppers and cook, stirring occasionally, until the tomatoes get juicy, 3 to 4 minutes.

4 Pour in the broth and coconut milk, add the chile peppers, and bring the broth to a simmer. Reduce the heat to medium-low and cover the pan. Cook the curry until the chicken is

¼ cup coconut milk

2 dried red chile peppers

3 tablespoons fresh lime juice

½ cup basil leaves (or even better, Thai basil leaves), stacked, rolled lengthwise, and sliced crosswise into thin ribbons

Steamed long-grain rice, for serving

cooked through and the peppers are tender, 25 to 30 minutes. Remove the lid and continue to cook to reduce the sauce slightly, about 5 minutes, then pour in the lime juice and cook for 30 seconds just to let the flavors come together. Turn off the heat and fish out the lime leaf, chile peppers, and garlic clove (if you can find it). Stir in the basil, and serve over rice.

Curried Flavors

I grew up eating curries in Indian restaurants and also at home. I add curry powder to so many dishes—like in my Garden Quiche (page 26) and the spice rub for my Herbed Crown Roast of Lamb (page 37). It's less about mimicking an "Indian" flavor and more about adding a hint of warmth and glow. On my travels I always will try the curry on a menu, whether I'm in Indonesia, where the spicy curry is scented with makrut lime leaves and lemongrass, or Japan, where the curry is sweet and creamy. I also love the spicy, coconutty curries of the Caribbean, the highly aromatic green and yellow curries of Thailand, and, of course, the myriad Indian curries that I tasted while living in London.

VEAL MARSALA *Serves 4*

8 veal cutlets (about 1¼ pounds)

1 teaspoon kosher salt

½ teaspoon freshly ground black pepper

2 tablespoons unsalted butter

1 tablespoon extra-virgin olive oil

3 small shallots, finely chopped

3 medium garlic cloves, minced

6 ounces mushrooms, stems trimmed and mushrooms thinly sliced

1 teaspoon finely chopped fresh rosemary

1 teaspoon finely chopped fresh thyme

½ cup Marsala wine

¾ cup beef broth

I had the most incredible veal Marsala one very hot summer evening in Sicily—it was so hot, in fact, that olive trees were actually combusting into flames as we drove past the groves! I can't explain why it happened—it just seemed *biblical*. We stopped in Taormina, a city close to Mt. Etna, where the early evening air was filled with the aroma of jasmine. The fortified flavor of sherry-like Marsala in the mushroom sauce completely perfumed the entire sensory experience. Afterward we walked to the outskirts of town and watched a ballet company rehearse in an ancient Greek amphitheater with the sun setting in the background. Some enchanted evening.

1 Set a veal cutlet on a piece of plastic wrap and cover with another sheet of plastic wrap. Use a meat mallet (a heavy-bottomed skillet works, too) to flatten the cutlet until it is about ⅛" thick. Place the cutlet on a plate and repeat with the remaining cutlets, then season with ½ teaspoon of the salt and the pepper.

2 Add 1 tablespoon of the butter and the olive oil to a large heavy-bottomed skillet and melt the butter over medium-high heat. Add a few cutlets (you will have to fry them in batches, so don't crowd the pan) and brown on both sides, about 1½ to 2 minutes per side, then transfer the cutlets to a large plate. Repeat with the remaining cutlets.

3 Stir in the shallots and garlic and cook, stirring often, until the shallots soften, about 3 minutes. Add the mushrooms and the remaining ½ teaspoon of salt and cook, stirring occasionally, until the mushrooms release their liquid and soften, 3 to 5 minutes. Stir in the rosemary and thyme, then immediately pour in the Marsala wine. Simmer until the wine is reduced by half, 2 to 3 minutes.

4 Pour the beef broth into the skillet and cook until it has reduced slightly, 3 to 4 minutes. Return the cutlets to the pan and use a spoon to coat them in the sauce. Use tongs to transfer the cutlets to a platter, then finish the sauce with the remaining 1 tablespoon of butter. Taste and add more salt or pepper if needed, then pour the sauce over the cutlets and serve.

MIXED BERRY GALETTE

Serves 4 to 6

3 cups mixed berries

¼ cup light brown sugar

1 tablespoon fresh lemon juice

1 tablespoon cornstarch

2 pinches of kosher salt

1 large egg

½ recipe My Favorite Pie Dough (page 50) or 1 round store-bought pie dough (not shaped in a tin)

Coarse sanding sugar, for sprinkling

Ice cream, for serving

BRUNCH WITH LENA

Some of the best kitchen discoveries come about through total kitchen disasters. I was planning a brunch for actor/director/author/activist Lena Dunham, one of my pals from our SoHo days, and was making this all-out ensemble of dishes. I went to the green market and bought a few baskets of the most beautiful summer berries to make a summer berry pie. I returned home and proceeded to shatter my pie dish on my Moroccan-tile kitchen floor! Disaster! Guests were minutes away from showing up, and I had to think fast. So instead of a pie, I improvised and we ended up with this wonderfully gorgeous, rustic, and free-form tart called a galette that doesn't require a pie dish. Everyone loved it—its nonconforming appearance and stunning quirks are what make it so special.

1 Preheat the oven to 425°F. Line a rimmed sheet pan with a nonstick baking mat or a piece of parchment paper.

2 Lightly toss the berries, brown sugar, lemon juice, cornstarch, and a pinch of salt together in a large bowl and set aside. Whisk the egg with a pinch of salt and 1 teaspoon of water in a small bowl.

3 Place the pie dough on the prepared sheet pan. Scoop up the berries and place them in the center of the dough. Leave a 2" border around the edges of the dough and use a pastry brush to lightly coat the border with some of the egg wash. Begin to fold the dough over the outer edge of the berries, pleating the dough as you go and leaving the center portion of the berries exposed. Brush the surface of the dough with the egg wash and sprinkle with the sanding sugar.

4 Bake the galette until the dough is golden brown, 20 to 25 minutes. Cool for at least 30 minutes before slicing and serving warm or at room temperature along with some ice cream.

BROWNED BUTTER-CHOCOLATE CHIP COOKIES *Makes 2 dozen cookies*

1 cup (2 sticks) unsalted butter

2½ cups all-purpose flour

1 teaspoon baking soda

½ teaspoon fine sea salt

1 cup lightly packed light brown sugar

½ cup granulated sugar

2 large eggs

½ vanilla bean, split lengthwise (optional)

1 teaspoon vanilla extract (increase to 2 teaspoons if not using the vanilla bean)

1½ cups semisweet chocolate chips

Flaky salt, such as fleur de sel (optional)

I ask you: What is there *not* to love about a cookie that is wonderfully soft in the middle, crisp around the edges, and has brown sugar all the way through? In my version of chocolate chip cookies, I cook the butter until it browns and becomes deep mahogany with a hazelnut scent, then chill it down. Only *then* do I use the chilled brown butter to make the cookies. It's an extra step, yes, but with so many cookies in the world, it's the fine touches that count—like a perfect handmade buttonhole on a suit that makes yours stand out from the crowd. Individually pressing some of the chips into the top of the cookie before baking gives these a polished and professional look. You can make and refrigerate the browned butter a week or two before making the cookies.

1 Add the butter to a medium saucepan (it's best to use one with a light-colored interior) and melt it slowly, swirling the butter often, over medium heat. Reduce the heat to medium-low and continue to let the butter cook, swirling occasionally to prevent the milk solids from burning, until the butter smells nutty and turns chestnut colored, 5 to 8 minutes. Turn off the heat and transfer the browned butter to a heat-safe bowl or liquid measuring cup and refrigerate until solid and chilled (it needs 1 to 2 hours to re-solidify).

2 Preheat the oven to 350°F. Line a rimmed sheet pan with parchment paper. Whisk the flour, baking soda, and sea salt together in a medium bowl and set aside. Add the butter to a large bowl or the bowl of a stand mixer fitted with the paddle attachment. Add the brown sugar and granulated sugar and use a wooden spoon to cream until the mixture is creamy and airy. If using a stand mixer, beat the mixture on medium speed until it is light and airy, about 1½ minutes.

recipe continues

3 Add the eggs, one at a time, beating well after each addition and using a rubber spatula to scrape the bottom and sides of the bowl as needed. If using a vanilla bean, use the tip of a paring knife to scrape away the vanilla seeds (drop the bean into a container of sugar to make vanilla sugar) and add them to the bowl along with the vanilla extract, mixing to combine.

4 Add the flour mixture and mix until no dry streaks remain (if using a stand mixer, add the flour on low speed and then increase the speed to medium-low until well combined), scraping the bottom and sides of the bowl as needed. Add a heaping 1 cup of the chocolate chips and stir to combine.

5 Use your hands to divide the dough into balls the size of golf balls. Place 12 balls on the prepared sheet pan and press some of the remaining chocolate chips on top (this will flatten the ball slightly). Sprinkle a little flaky salt (if using) over each cookie (at this point, the cookies can be held in the refrigerator for up to 3 days—they will have an even richer flavor and chewy texture from aging in the fridge). Bake until the cookies are golden brown around the edges, about 12 minutes (they will still feel a bit soft in the center but will continue to cook as they cool on the sheet pan). Cool for 5 minutes, then transfer the cookies to a wire rack to cool completely. Repeat with the remaining dough. Obviously, they are delicious served warm.

Baking in the Berkshires

I've loved to bake for as long as I can remember and always looked forward to visiting my godmother in the Berkshires on long weekends because she, too, loved to bake, and she always insisted that I help. Whenever we baked cookies, she would cover a long Nakashima-like table with brown paper bags cut open to lie flat, and we'd place the baked chocolate chip cookies fresh from the oven on the brown paper to absorb the extra oil from them as they cooled. We functioned like an assembly line, baking off tray after tray of cookies. I have no idea who ate them all! I always think of her every time I bake a dozen.

KELP TEA *Serves 2*

3 pieces (each 4" long) dried kombu

4 cups water

You can get kombu at most health food stores or order it online. Choose leaves that are deep green and wide—these are the innermost sections of the kelp leaves and have the most flavor and nutrients. Kelp is great for your immune system and so good for digestion. Its natural minerals help deliver oxygen to blood cells. Drink as tea, use alone as a broth, or use as the base for Dashi Broth (page 136).

1 Place the kombu in a medium pot (break the pieces to fit in the pot if needed) and add the water. Bring the water to a gentle simmer over medium heat (don't let it boil).

2 Reduce the heat to medium-low and gently simmer the kombu for 30 minutes. Turn off the heat. You can let the kombu cool in the water and then discard it, or discard the kombu immediately and drink the tea warm.

Jush Your Kelp Tea

The recipe above is for your very basic, clean kombu tea, which I love. But sometimes, I like to add a few extras in step 2. Here are just a few ideas.

- Smashed lemongrass
- Slices of fresh ginger
- Dried red chile peppers
- Lime juice
- Scored shiitake mushrooms
- Handful of bonito flakes
- Soy sauce
- Shiso leaves

ORANGE BLOSSOM BUNDT CAKE *Serves 10 to 12*

1 cup (2 sticks) plus
2 tablespoons unsalted
butter, at room
temperature

3 cups all-purpose
flour, plus
2 tablespoons
for the pan

1 teaspoon baking
powder

¼ teaspoon baking
soda

¼ teaspoon fine
sea salt

2¾ cups granulated
sugar

5 large eggs

1 teaspoon vanilla
extract

½ teaspoon almond
extract

1 cup sour cream

1 teaspoon finely
grated lemon zest, plus
the juice of 1 lemon

1 teaspoon finely
grated orange zest,
plus freshly squeezed
orange juice
(combined with the
lemon juice, it should
come to ½ cup)

1 tablespoon orange
blossom water or rose
water

When you host guests for weekends at a country house, everyone falls into a wonderfully relaxed and mellow state of being—it's really the best thing about being in the country, just the gift of recharging after an intense week in the city. As a host to weekend guests, it's important to have a handful of simple, no-fuss yet delicious and elegant recipes at the ready. That way, the morning can be for relaxing, enjoying a cup of coffee and light and leisurely conversation. Slices of this Bundt cake make a great afternoon snack, smeared with jam and topped with a dollop of whipped cream, or even pan-fried in some butter and served with a dusting of powdered sugar.

1 Preheat the oven to 350°F. Coat a Bundt pan with the 2 tablespoons of softened butter, then add the 2 tablespoons of flour and shake to evenly coat the pan, tapping out the excess over the sink. Whisk the remaining 3 cups of flour, the baking powder, baking soda, and salt together in a medium bowl and set aside.

2 Add the remaining 1 cup of butter and 2½ cups of the sugar to the bowl of a stand mixer fitted with a paddle attachment and cream together on medium-low speed until combined, about 15 seconds. Increase the speed to medium-high and cream until the mixture is very light, creamy, and airy, about 3 minutes, using a rubber spatula to scrape the bottom and sides of the bowl as needed.

3 Reduce the mixer speed to medium-low and add the eggs one at a time, beating for 20 seconds after each addition and stopping the mixer to scrape the sides and bottom of the bowl as needed. Add the vanilla and almond extracts and beat to combine. Add one-third of the flour mixture, mixing until only a few dry streaks remain. Mix in half of the sour cream, followed by half of the remaining flour mixture, the remaining sour cream, and finally the rest of the flour mixture. Mix for 15 seconds or until well combined, stopping the mixer to scrape the sides and bottom of the bowl as needed.

4 Use a rubber spatula to scrape the batter into the prepared Bundt pan as evenly as possible. Place the spatula under cool running water for a second and then use the wet spatula to smooth out the top of the cake. Bake the cake until it is golden brown and resists light pressure and a cake tester inserted into the center of the cake comes out clean, about 1 hour and 15 minutes (if the top of the cake begins to brown too much, lightly tent it with a sheet of aluminum foil).

5 Remove the cake from the oven and place it on a wire rack to cool for 30 minutes. Turn the pan over onto the rack and tap it a few times to remove the cake from the pan. Let it cool for 15 minutes.

6 Meanwhile, make the glaze: Whisk the remaining ¼ cup of sugar, the lemon and orange juices, zests, and the orange blossom water together in a medium bowl until the sugar is dissolved. Use a pastry brush to dab the top of the cake with the syrup, allowing it to seep in. Slice and serve.

Quick Lemon Glaze

A simple lemon glaze made with powdered sugar and lemon juice instantly transforms cookies, cakes, and muffins into a more polished-looking bakery-worthy treat. Simply whisk 1 cup of sifted powdered sugar (sifting is important so your icing is silky smooth) with 3 tablespoons of lemon juice until it drips from the whisk in thick ribbons. For a thinner glaze, add a teaspoon more of lemon juice, and for a thicker glaze, add a few more tablespoons of powdered sugar. For a more opaque-white glaze, use heavy cream or buttermilk with a little lemon juice for tartness. While the glaze is tacky, you can sprinkle finely grated lemon zest, chopped nuts, or toasted coconut over the top of whatever treat you've made.

CASTELLA SPONGE CAKE

Makes two 8" loaves (you will need two disposable 8" loaf pans)

6 large eggs, at room temperature

1 cup granulated sugar

½ vanilla bean, split lengthwise

7 tablespoons honey

1 cup bread flour, sifted 2 times

½ teaspoon grated lemon zest, plus 2 tablespoons lemon juice (preferably Meyer lemon)

Pinch of sea salt

Fresh berries, for serving

Sweetened whipped cream, for serving

My mom used to work crazy hours during the week, but on the weekend, she put on her apron and baked up a storm. I'd stand by her side and see if I could help. This Japanese sponge cake recipe made with a few spare ingredients is one of my go-to recipes. It is *critical* that the eggs be at room temperature, so don't skip that step! Room temperature eggs whip up frothier and creamier, making your sponge light and airy. Also, be sure to use bread flour and not all-purpose flour. If you make the cake with all-purpose flour, it will sink in the middle. The texture of the cake is best when made in this size batch— when the recipe is halved, the texture just isn't the same. Lucky you . . . two cakes are always better than one! I use disposable loaf pans, which makes it easy to freeze one cake or give one away. Note that the cakes need to be refrigerated for 12 hours before serving.

1 Preheat the oven to 325°F. Spray two disposable 8" loaf pans with nonstick cooking spray. Trim two pieces of parchment paper to 14" x 8" and place them crosswise in the pans so the edges hang over the long sides of the loaf pans. Trim two more pieces of parchment to 12" x 4½" and place them in the pans (overlapping the first pieces) lengthwise. Spray the parchment with nonstick cooking spray.

2 Add the eggs and sugar to the bowl of a stand mixer fitted with the whisk attachment (or add them to a large bowl if using a hand mixer) and beat on medium speed until frothy, about 1 minute. Increase the mixer speed to high and beat until the eggs are very voluminous and have roughly quadrupled in volume, about 5 minutes (when you lift the whisk, the egg mixture should fall from the attachment in heavy ribbons).

recipe continues

3   Use a paring knife to scrape the vanilla seeds out of the bean and add them to the egg mixture (add the bean to a container of sugar to infuse it with vanilla essence). Mix 5 tablespoons of the honey with 2½ tablespoons of warm water in a small bowl until well combined. Add the honey mixture to the mixer bowl along with the flour, lemon zest, and salt. Beat on medium speed until combined and no dry streaks remain, about 15 seconds.

4   Use a rubber spatula to divide the batter among the prepared loaf pans. Use a toothpick or cake tester to make zigzags through the batter to eliminate any air bubbles. Smooth out the tops and bake the cakes until the tops are deeply browned, the cakes pull away from the sides of the pans, and the centers bounce back to light pressure, 35 to 40 minutes. Set the cakes (still in the pans) aside on a wire rack.

5   While the cake is baking, mix the remaining 2 tablespoons of honey with the lemon juice and 2 tablespoons of warm water in a small bowl until well combined. While the cakes are warm, brush the honey mixture over each cake, then pop the cakes out from the pans. Leave the parchment on the cakes and wrap each one tightly in parchment paper. Refrigerate them top side down for 12 hours. Let the cake sit at room temperature for 15 minutes before unwrapping. Use a serrated knife to slice away the browned edges from the cake (they make a great snack). Slice the cake crosswise into 1"-wide pieces and serve with berries and whipped cream.

Make One, Freeze One

A great host always has a sweet thing tucked away somewhere (in a cupboard, in the freezer, in a cookie jar) to offer drop-in guests with their coffee, tea, or aperitivo. *Since this recipe yields two cakes, simply wrap the extra one in a layer of plastic wrap, place it in a gallon-size freezer bag, and freeze for up to 3 months. It defrosts at room temperature in just an hour or two depending on the warmth of the room.*

LAVENDER SUGAR COOKIES *Makes 2½ dozen cookies*

2½ cups all-purpose flour

½ teaspoon baking powder

½ teaspoon kosher salt

½ teaspoon fresh lavender or ¼ teaspoon dried

Finely grated zest of ½ lemon

1½ cups granulated sugar

1 cup (2 sticks) unsalted butter, at room temperature

1 large egg

¼ teaspoon lavender extract

¼ teaspoon vanilla extract

1½ cups coarse sanding sugar

There is something so romantic about combining flower essences and herbs into sweet dishes. The flavor of the flower is there, and it's nostalgic and relaxing all at once. These cookies bake up like sweet sparkly clouds, and paired with lavender, they're positively fanciful.

1 Preheat the oven to 375°F. Whisk the flour, baking powder, and salt together in a medium bowl and set aside. Very finely chop the lavender and lemon zest together and add it to a small bowl with the granulated sugar. Use your fingers to work the lavender and lemon zest into the sugar until the sugar looks sandy and is fragrant.

2 Add the butter to the bowl of a stand mixer fitted with the paddle attachment and cream on medium speed until very creamy, about 2 minutes. Use a rubber spatula to scrape the bottom and sides of the bowl, then add the sugar and continue to cream until the mixture is pale and airy, about 2 minutes longer.

3 Add the egg and extracts and continue to cream together until well combined, stopping the mixer to scrape the bottom and sides of the bowl as needed. Reduce the mixer speed to low and add the flour mixture. Increase the speed to medium-low and cream until well combined, about 1 minute.

4 Add the sanding sugar to a medium bowl. Divide the dough into balls the size of Ping-Pong balls, then roll each in the sanding sugar before placing on a parchment paper–lined sheet pan, spacing them about 1½" apart to allow room to spread.

5 Bake the cookies until they are just starting to become golden at the edges but are still quite pale on top, 9 to 12 minutes. Remove from the oven and cool for 5 minutes, then transfer to a wire rack to cool completely. Repeat with the remaining dough (or freeze the dough balls to bake off another time, see page 231). Store in an airtight container for up to 1 week.

MINTY MELON ICE *Serves 8*

1 cup granulated sugar

4 sprigs fresh mint, plus 8 small sprigs for serving

6 cups frozen 1" honeydew melon cubes

In New York City, an Italian ice is called an icy, and it's *the best* on a swelteringly hot and steamy summer day. I especially love the cherry flavor that leaves my tongue bright red! Here I make a blender ice slush that requires very little time or effort (and no ice cream maker, making it a perfect weekend at the beach go-to), with herbs for a hint of the unexpected. Mint and honeydew are incredibly refreshing and instantly translate into something chic and elegant. Plus, since the ice is dairy-free and fat-free, it's easy to serve to friends with dietary restrictions. I like serving it simply in a beautiful antique dessert cup—it gives the dessert loads of charm. You can always serve it in the style of Italian lemon sorbet, too: piled high into a frozen lemon half. It's also delicious made with some tequila or Prosecco instead of water.

1   Bring the sugar and ½ cup of water to a boil in a small saucepan, stirring often. Boil until the sugar dissolves, 2 to 3 minutes. Add the mint, cover the pan, and set aside to cool, at least 10 minutes. Remove and discard the mint and add 1 cup of cold water to the mint syrup.

2   Add the melon and mint syrup to a blender and purée until thick and slushy. Divide among eight small dessert glasses and serve garnished with a mint sprig and a spoon or a straw.

FALL &
WINTER

Fall is far and away my favorite season for fashion because the design elements include layering and the fabrics involve textures and interesting knits. The looks are typically more intricate than pieces from other fashion seasons. I feel the same way about the food that I make in the fall. Instead of a simple fresh-from-the-garden pasta or a quick simmer-and-purée spring soup, I'm craving warmth and coziness via the comforting and complex flavors of stews and roasts.

Also as soon as the fall season arrives, as if by clockwork, I kick into action and start baking like crazy. I think it's kind of like getting ready for hibernation and preparing for cold winters. I seem to come up with lots of new ideas and dishes in the late fall when I have the time to experiment. The aromas from a long-cooking roast with its accompanying herbs coupled with a cake or cookies baking in the oven make me exceptionally happy. I can even tell by the smell coming from the oven whether my baking is done!

Starting in September, the atelier gets cooking, too. During this time period, we are preparing for our Fall Collection, which is presented on the runway in the early weeks of February. The fabrics for my Fall Collection often include cashmere coating, suiting, duchesse satin, crisp silk faille, patterned jacquards, and lush velvets. Out of these ingredients I sculpt, tailor, and mold using intricate techniques to form the suits, dresses, and gowns. The superbusy hive of activity in the atelier at the year's end always reminds me of what I imagine Santa's workshop must be like! On Instagram, my followers have often tagged the atelier as #wherethemagichappens, and I couldn't agree more, because magic seems to happen where your love and passion reside, and for me, that's in the atelier and in the kitchen. Cooking delicious meals and creating beautiful things to wear are how I like to create magic.

FALL & WINTER

MY BIRTHDAY MUSHROOM TOAST

Serves 8 to 10

4 tablespoons
unsalted butter

10 garlic cloves,
very thinly sliced

12 ounces porcini,
shiitake, or cremini
(brown) mushrooms,
stems removed and
caps thinly sliced

1 teaspoon fine sea
salt, plus more to taste

2 teaspoons finely
chopped fresh
rosemary leaves

2 teaspoons finely
chopped fresh thyme
leaves

2 dried bay leaves

1 teaspoon freshly
ground black pepper,
plus more to taste

½ cup heavy cream

2 tablespoons finely
chopped fresh flat-leaf
parsley

6 slices (½"–¾" thick)
brioche (or use any
bread you like—I love
the buttery taste of
brioche), toasted and
cut into 2" squares
(2–3 bites per toast)

Wedge of Parmigiano-
Reggiano cheese,
for grating

I am notorious for choosing *not* to celebrate my birthday (which comes at the end of October). I prefer to lie low, maybe cook for some friends, and be very mellow and casual about it. My friend Masha brought me the most beautiful birthday gift for my 36th birthday—a basketful of cèpe (porcini) mushrooms that she foraged for in the woods of Maine. With mushrooms you have to be extra careful—not only are there poisonous ones out and about, but there are "magical" mushrooms, too! Usually I might err on the side of safety, but I know Masha, and she knows what she is doing, so I decided to turn the fragrant, wild-looking creatures into a rich topping for toasts (and I'm happy to report that no one had any crazy mushroom-induced birthday prophecies!). Not everyone has someone like Masha in their lives to deliver fresh-foraged mushrooms—so substitute shiitakes or brown mushrooms if you must.

1 Melt the butter in a large skillet over medium heat, swirling it often, until it is lightly browned and toasty smelling, about 3 minutes.

2 Stir in the garlic and cook until fragrant, 1 to 2 minutes, then stir in the mushrooms and the salt. Cook, stirring occasionally, until the mushrooms become glossy, 2 to 3 minutes. Reduce the heat to medium-low and stir in the rosemary, thyme, bay leaves, and pepper. Continue to cook until the mushrooms are very glossy, shriveled, and just starting to brown, about 15 minutes (they should be at a soft, gentle sizzle the whole time).

3 Stir in the cream, cook for 1 minute, then turn off the heat and stir in the parsley. Taste and adjust with additional salt and pepper as needed. Remove and discard the bay leaves.

4 Arrange the toasted brioche on a platter and spoon the mushroom mixture on top. Grate some Parmigiano-Reggiano cheese over the top and serve. The mushrooms can be prepared up to 2 days ahead of time and rewarmed before serving.

DASHI BROTH *Makes about 7 cups*

12 kombu (seaweed) strips (each 6" long)

8 large fresh shiitake mushroom caps

4 large handfuls (about 4 lightly packed cups) bonito flakes

½ cup dried small sardines (available in Asian markets)

Just as there are infinite varieties of chicken soup, there are many ways to make dashi, the Japanese broth that is used to make traditional miso soup. High in umami flavor, bonito flakes are essential for a traditional dashi (but if making a vegetarian dashi, you can leave them out; add a few tablespoons of miso paste after straining for a savory taste)—they are thinly shaved petals of dried and fermented fish, often tuna or sometimes mackerel. Along with Japanese kelp seaweed called kombu, they are the two critical components for making dashi. I like a little extra savory-umami flavor from tiny dried sardines, but they can be left out.

1 Add the kombu and 8 cups of cold water to a large pot and warm gently over medium heat until steam rises off the top of the pot (you don't want the water to boil or simmer). As white foam rises to the top, skim it off (this can make the dashi bitter, so it is good to remove it from the liquid). Once you see steam rising off the top, turn off the heat, cover the pot, and let the kombu sit in the water for 40 minutes.

2 Use a slotted spoon to remove the kombu. Bring the liquid to a simmer over medium heat. Use the tip of a paring knife to slice an asterisk in the top of each mushroom cap (make an *X* and then add another slit across the center). Reduce the heat to medium-low and add the bonito, sardines, and shiitakes to the broth. Continue to gently simmer until the sardines are semi-soft (but not falling apart), about 20 minutes.

3 Use a slotted spoon to remove the shiitakes and set them aside (you can slice them and return them to the strained broth or add them to a stir-fry). Strain the dashi through a cheesecloth or fine-mesh sieve lined with paper towels, pressing on the solids lightly to extract as much of the broth as possible (discard the solids). Return the mushrooms to the broth (if desired) and serve warm, or refrigerate the dashi for up to 5 days.

Say What? Kombu!

Kombu is a seaweed often sold under the name kelp (see page 119 for my Kelp Tea recipe). It is sold dried either in long, wide strips or in small squares. Kombu (also called dashima in Korean) contains natural glutamic acid, the base of MSG (a chemically modified version of glutamic acid along with other components). Like MSG, natural glutamic acid—the white powder often seen on the surface of the dried kombu—adds a savory and softly salty taste to foods. It also tenderizes proteins, which is why many people like to add a strip or two to a pot of dried beans as they simmer. Once simmered, kombu softens and can actually dissolve right into hot liquid. If you take it out before it completely breaks down, you can cut it into strips and chill it to eat in salads (kelp is often called a sea vegetable, after all!) or just snack on it plain, which is what I like to do. (Kelp is a great source of natural iodine, which is good for your thyroid and metabolism.) Since too much of anything is never good, after snacking on a piece or two, I'll save the rest for composting since it also offers fantastic nutrition for flowers and plants.

RAMEN WITH LIME AND LEMONGRASS *Serves 4*

6 cups Dashi Broth (page 136)

½ cup shoyu (Japanese soy sauce) (see page 80)

½ cup mirin rice wine

½ cup cooking sake

2 stalks lemongrass, tough outer layer removed, stalk sliced into thirds, and inner reed smashed with a knife

1½ pounds (24 ounces) fresh ramen noodles or 4 packages (3 ounces each) instant ramen (discard the spice packets)

1 tablespoon freshly grated gingerroot

2 soft- to medium-cooked eggs (depending on your preference; see page 140), peeled and halved

3 scallions, dark green and white parts, thinly sliced

1 lime, cut into wedges

I have always been wild for ramen noodles. When I was old enough to travel around New York City on my own, I tried many of the East Village ramen shops, sitting at counters (as one does) trying out their ramen. It wasn't until I traveled to Japan that I experienced the true art of ramen when I tasted how subtle and varied ramen could be. From that point forward, I chucked the seasoning package that comes with packaged ramen and replaced it with great Japanese seasoning from dashi to miso. This is what I do here—if your ramen comes with a seasoning packet, don't feel guilty about pitching it and making your own delicious spiced broth.

1 Add the dashi, shoyu, mirin, sake, and lemongrass to a large saucepan and bring it to a simmer over low heat—this takes a while, but the slow infusion creates more flavor.

2 Add the ramen noodles and cook according to the package instructions. Turn off the heat and stir in the ginger. Divide the soup among four bowls (discard the lemongrass). Add an egg half to each bowl, sprinkle with scallions, and serve with a lime wedge.

A PERFECT SOFT/MEDIUM/ HARD-COOKED EGG

Different dishes call for varying degrees of hard-boiled yolks—sometimes, like with ramen soup, you want a semi-soft yolk; for deviled eggs, you want a cooked yet still creamy yolk; for egg salad, you want a hard yolk. Here's a quick guide to getting that perfect yolk every time.

1. Let your eggs come to room temperature so they are less likely to crack once they are submerged in the hot water (or place the eggs in a bowl of warm water to lose their chill).

2. Bring a saucepan of water to a boil then reduce the heat so the water is at a medium simmer (boiling eggs will lead to a rubbery egg white and could potentially crack the shell).

3. Use a slotted spoon to lower the egg into the water. Let it gently roll off the spoon.

COOKING TIMES

6 minutes: very soft white and a barely cooked yolk (this one can be tricky to peel!)

7 minutes: semi-firm white and a yolk with a soft core and creamy-set edges (great for ramen soup!)

8 minutes: firm white and a firm yet still creamy-tasting yolk (great for deviled eggs, or for ramen if you prefer a more set yolk)

9 minutes: firm white and a firm yolk (great for any recipe calling for a crumbly yet not dry yolk)

10 minutes: firm white and a hard ball yolk (nice for egg salads)

11 minutes: very firm and hard (for egg salads or potato salads)

2 tablespoons vegetable oil

1½ pounds 2"-thick oxtail segments (buy at least 1 oxtail segment per serving)

2 teaspoons fine sea salt

1 teaspoon freshly ground black pepper

3 medium garlic cloves, peeled and smashed

1 star anise pod

1 cinnamon stick

1 large leek, green tops discarded, cleaned, halved lengthwise, and thinly sliced

1 large carrot, peeled and sliced into ½"-thick pieces

1 large parsnip, peeled and sliced into ½"-thick pieces

1 medium turnip, peeled and cut into ½"–¾" pieces

½ medium yellow onion, finely chopped

1 teaspoon finely chopped gingerroot

1 fresh or dried bay leaf

1 teaspoon ground cumin

1 cup canned chopped tomatoes

2 tablespoons soy sauce

2 quarts (8 cups) beef broth

1 sprig fresh thyme

½ cup medium pearled barley (not instant)

¼ cup chopped cilantro

1 lime, cut into wedges

OXTAIL–BARLEY SOUP

Serves 6 to 8

Think beef barley soup. Now think of the *best* beef barley soup, and you're in the zone of oxtails. Like short ribs, they must be cooked for a very long time to encourage the meat to fall from the bone, and once it does, you're in business! The flavor and richness they lend to a broth is just unparalleled. I've added a few tweaks to the classic version, like a squeeze of lime juice to cut through the richness and cilantro for its fresh taste.

1 Heat the vegetable oil in a large heavy-bottomed pot over medium-high heat. Sprinkle the oxtails with salt and pepper and then set them into the hot oil. Cook until browned on the bottom, 5 to 7 minutes, then use tongs to turn them over.

2 Add the garlic, star anise, and cinnamon and cook until the garlic is fragrant, about 30 seconds. Add the leek, carrot, parsnip, turnip, onion, ginger, bay leaf, and cumin and stir to combine. Stir in the tomatoes and soy sauce, then add the broth and thyme.

3 Increase the heat to high. Once the liquid comes to a low boil, reduce the heat to medium-low, cover, and gently simmer for 2 hours, stirring every 30 minutes. Stir in the barley and continue to cook until the oxtail meat easily falls off the bone, about 1 to 1½ hours longer (the oxtails will cook for 3 to 3½ hours total). Remove and discard the star anise, cinnamon stick, bay leaf, and thyme sprig.

4 Taste and add more salt or pepper if needed. Divide into bowls, making sure each bowl gets an oxtail segment. Sprinkle with the cilantro and serve with a lime wedge on the side.

DASHI-GLAZED LOTUS ROOT AND WINTER VEGETABLES *Serves 4*

2 cups Dashi Broth (page 136), plus reserved shiitake mushrooms (optional)

2 tablespoons mirin rice wine

¼ cup soy sauce

1 tablespoon cooking sake (or extra mirin)

1 tablespoon granulated sugar

1 tablespoon canola or vegetable oil

1 large yellow onion, chopped

1 piece (1½" long) fresh gingerroot, peeled, thinly sliced lengthwise, stacked, and cut into thin strips

1 very large, thick carrot, peeled and sliced on a bias into ½"-thick pieces

1 medium lotus root (about ¾ pound), ends removed, peeled, and cut crosswise into ½"-thick slices

1 pound winter squash (my favorite is kabocha), halved, seeded, peeled, and cut into 1½"–2" pieces

2 shiso leaves, stacked, rolled lengthwise, and sliced crosswise into thin ribbons (optional)

4 whole pickled plums (also called *umeboshi*, optional)

After making dashi, many savvy Japanese cooks strain out the vegetables, then chill and save them. These vegetables are infused with the savory umami taste of the dashi, so why pitch them? For extra sweetness and shine, soy sauce, cooking sake, and mirin are added to the vegetables. Just like that, from one dish you've created two! So economical, practical, and above all healthy. In this version, lotus root is the star. It holds up well to cooking, and while it doesn't offer much in flavor, like tofu, it is a great flavor carrier and adds tremendous visual appeal and a nice crunch to any dish. Shiso leaves (sometimes called perilla) taste like a cross between cilantro and basil; you can find them, and pickled plums, in Asian markets.

---

1 Pour the dashi into a medium saucepan and add the mirin, soy sauce, sake, and sugar. Bring to a simmer over medium heat and then continue to simmer for 2 minutes to let the flavors come together. Set aside.

2 Heat the canola or vegetable oil in a large heavy-bottomed pot over medium-high heat. Add the onion and cook until it starts to brown, stirring often, about 5 minutes. Stir in the ginger and once it becomes fragrant, after 30 seconds or so, add the carrot followed by the lotus root. Pour in the seasoned dashi (it should rise about halfway up the vegetables) and bring to a simmer.

3 Reduce the heat to medium-low, cover, and cook until the carrot is tender, about 15 minutes. Add the squash and reserved shiitakes (if using). Cook, covered, for 20 minutes longer. Uncover the pan and continue to cook, using a spoon to drizzle the glaze from the pot over the top of the vegetables, until the squash is tender, 5 to 10 minutes longer.

4 Divide the vegetables among four bowls. Add some dashi to each. Sprinkle with the shiso leaves (if using) and serve with a pickled plum (if using).

MISO–ROASTED SQUASH

Serves 4

1 large squash (my favorite is kabocha; about 1¾–2 pounds), well scrubbed, halved, seeded, and cut into wedges

¼ cup red miso paste

2 tablespoons extra-virgin olive oil

2 teaspoons yuzu juice, or 1 teaspoon lemon juice plus 1 teaspoon orange juice

6 medium garlic cloves, minced

2 tablespoons granulated sugar

2 teaspoons fine sea salt

½ teaspoon freshly ground black pepper

⅛ teaspoon finely grated fresh nutmeg

If your knowledge of winter squash is confined to butternut and acorn, then you have the wonderful world of winter squash to explore—like sweet and dense kabocha, savory calabaza, and mild delicata. I like to cut the squash, seed it, and then slice it into wedges for roasting. With many squash varieties like red kuri, kabocha, buttercup, and acorn squash, the skin becomes tender enough during roasting that you don't even need to peel it. If using butternut or Hubbard squash, then you definitely want to remove the skin before roasting.

1 Preheat the oven to 400°F and line a rimmed sheet pan with aluminum foil. Place the squash wedges on top.

2 Mix together the miso paste, olive oil, yuzu juice, garlic, sugar, salt, pepper, and nutmeg in a small bowl.

3 Add the miso mixture to the squash and toss until coated. Place the squash wedges on a flat side and roast for 25 minutes, then turn the pieces over and continue to roast until a paring knife easily slides through a wedge without meeting any resistance, about 20 minutes longer.

LEMON ZEST POMODORO *Serves 4*

2 tablespoons extra-virgin olive oil

4 large whole, peeled garlic cloves

1 teaspoon finely grated lemon zest

1 tablespoon tomato paste

¼ cup dry red wine (optional)

2½ cups canned diced or crushed tomatoes (from a 26-ounce box or can)

1 teaspoon granulated sugar

½ teaspoon fine sea salt, plus extra if needed

½ teaspoon freshly ground black pepper, plus extra if needed

2 large whole basil leaves, plus additional small leaves for serving

Cooked pasta or gnocchi (page 149)

In this recipe, I cook garlic slowly in oil to caramelize it and coax out its wonderfully deep and nutty flavor without risk of burning. The trick is to put the garlic in the oil before you start warming the oil in the pan. I learned this tip from none other than Chef Mario Batali, whom I met when I was in my early twenties and living a block from Babbo, his fabulous Italian restaurant in Greenwich Village. After the kitchen closed for the night, I'd sometimes bump into him and his crew on the stoop outside the restaurant. Years later Katie Holmes invited me to a cooking class he taught for her at Eataly; it was fun to reconnect with Mario after so many years! I sometimes add pitted olives or capers to this sauce to give it a briny bite.

1   Place the olive oil and garlic in a large deep skillet and set over low heat. Cook the garlic, moving it around occasionally, until it smells deeply toasty and is beginning to turn brown at the tips, 7 to 10 minutes. Use a fork to remove the garlic from the pan. (For a more pronounced garlic flavor, smash some or all of the garlic and add it to the sauce in step 2; otherwise, save the garlic for another use.)

2   Increase the heat to medium and add the lemon zest to the garlic-infused oil. Once it begins to smell fragrant, after 30 seconds to 1 minute, stir in the tomato paste. Once the tomato paste darkens, after 2 to 3 minutes, stir in the wine (if using). Add the tomatoes (if using diced tomatoes instead of crushed, use a potato masher to smash the tomatoes into the oil to smooth out the texture a bit) along with the sugar, salt, pepper, and basil. If using some smashed garlic, stir it in now.

3   Turn off the heat, taste, and add more salt or pepper if needed. Serve over pasta or gnocchi, garnished with small basil leaves.

1 tablespoon vegetable oil

1 large yellow onion, chopped into ¾" pieces

1 large carrot, ends trimmed, peeled, and halved lengthwise, then sliced on a diagonal into ½"- to ¾"-thick pieces

2 teaspoons fine sea salt, plus extra if needed

½ teaspoon freshly ground black pepper

1 tablespoon tomato paste

1½ cups shiitake mushrooms, stemmed and halved

1 medium russet potato, peeled and cut into ½"–¾" cubes

1 medium apple, halved, cored, and cut into ½"–¾" cubes

1 small sweet potato (preferably a white Japanese sweet potato), peeled and cut into ½"–¾" cubes

½ pound winter squash (I like kabocha squash), halved, seeded, peeled, and cut into ½"–¾" cubes

1 quart (4 cups) vegetable broth, Dashi Broth (page 136), or chicken broth (page 208)

2 tablespoons mirin rice wine

1 tablespoon soy sauce

ingredients continue

JAPANESE VEGETABLE CURRY *Serves 6*

I probably make this dish, which is somewhere between a stew and a thick curry, two or three times a month during the winter months. It's soul-satisfying goodness and deeply comforting, reminding me of Japan, a place I absolutely adore. This is a vegetarian curry, so it's on the lean side, too. Of course, I always make some rice to accompany the curry (see page 148 for Perfectly Sticky Brown Rice) because all that curry sauce begs for steamed rice. Bulgur or quinoa (page 172) are also great with this nourishing cold-weather meal.

1 *To make the vegetables:* Heat the vegetable oil in a large pot over medium-high heat. Add the onion, carrot, salt, and black pepper and stir to combine. Stir in the tomato paste and cook, stirring often, until the tomato paste darkens, 3 to 4 minutes. Add the mushrooms, potato, apple, sweet potato, and squash and stir to combine, then add the broth, mirin, and soy sauce. Increase the heat to high and bring to a simmer, then reduce the heat to medium-low, cover the pot, and cook the vegetables at a gentle simmer until they are tender, about 20 minutes.

2 *To make the roux:* Meanwhile, melt the butter in a small saucepan over medium-high heat. Add the onion and salt, reduce the heat to medium-low, and cook, stirring often, until the onion starts to soften, 5 to 6 minutes. Stir in the ginger and garlic and continue to cook, stirring occasionally, until the onion has melted into a somewhat pasty/grainy-looking mixture, about 15 minutes total. Stir in the curry powder, cinnamon, and chile pepper (if using), then stir in the flour. Continue to cook, stirring often, to give the flour a chance to lose its raw taste and brown in the fat, about 5 minutes.

3 Use a ladle to stir ½ cup of broth from the vegetables into the roux mixture. It will get absorbed quickly, so stir fast to

recipe continues

1 tablespoon honey

Finely chopped fresh
flat-leaf parsley or
basil, for serving

Roux

3 tablespoons unsalted
butter

1 small yellow onion,
very finely chopped

½ teaspoon fine
sea salt

2 teaspoons finely
grated fresh
gingerroot

1 medium garlic clove,
very finely chopped
or grated on a
Microplane-style rasp

2 tablespoons curry
powder or garam
masala

¼ teaspoon ground
cinnamon

½ small chile pepper
(such as a Scotch
bonnet, habanero,
or serrano), finely
chopped (optional)

½ cup all-purpose
flour

work out any lumps. Add another ½ cup of broth and stir. Continue until the roux mixture is pretty liquidy (perhaps another ½ to 1 cup of broth, depending on how much liquid your saucepan can handle). Scrape the roux into the pot with the vegetables and use a wooden spoon to stir it into the broth.

4 Simmer the curry until the liquid is thickened and glossy, about 10 minutes. Stir in the honey, then taste and add more salt if needed. Serve with parsley or basil.

Perfectly Sticky Brown Rice

Place 2 cups of short-grain brown rice in a bowl and cover with cold water. Soak the rice for 2 hours, then drain and set aside. Bring 3 cups of water to a boil in a medium saucepan. Add the soaked and drained rice and stir once. Return the water to a boil, then cover the saucepan, reduce the heat to low, and cook until the rice is tender, about 40 minutes. Turn off the heat and leave the pan covered to steam for 5 to 10 minutes before serving. (I like to lightly oil a teacup, pack the rice in, and invert the rice onto the plate—the cup gives it a perfectly "molded" presentation!)

POTATO–RICOTTA GNOCCHI *Serves 6*

1 cup whole-milk ricotta cheese

4 medium Yukon gold potatoes (1¾–2 pounds total), whole and unpeeled, pricked with a fork

¼ cup finely grated Parmigiano-Reggiano cheese, plus extra for serving

1½ teaspoons plus 2 tablespoons fine sea salt

1 large egg, lightly beaten

¾ cup all-purpose flour, plus extra for rolling and shaping

¾ cup cake flour or 00 flour

Semolina flour or fine cornmeal

1 recipe warm Lemon Zest Pomodoro (page 145) or your favorite homemade or store-bought marinara sauce

Small basil leaves, for serving

This is really a recipe that relies on senses rather than measurements—sometimes your flour is drier, the air is more humid, your eggs are larger, there is more water in your ricotta. That said, gnocchi are very forgiving at the same time; I think the best thing about them is the handmade aspect and variation from piece to piece (just like fashion, really). After making these light, tender gnocchi a few times, you'll have a natural sense of knowing the right texture and feel of the dough. I love them with the Lemon Zest Pomodoro on page 145, but they're also great with any tomato-based marinara or ragu.

1 Strain the ricotta for the gnocchi: Line a fine-mesh sieve with a double layer of cheesecloth and set it over a medium bowl. Place the ricotta in the sieve and set it aside to drain for 1 hour.

2 Boil the potatoes for the gnocchi: Bring a large pot of water to a boil. Add the potatoes, reduce the heat to medium, and gently boil until a paring knife easily slides into the center of a potato, about 20 minutes, depending on how large the potatoes are. Drain the potatoes and, once they are cool enough to handle, peel away the skin. (I like to save it for snacking.)

3 Cut the potatoes into quarters and push them through a potato ricer (or food mill) and into a medium bowl. Add the strained ricotta, the Parmigiano-Reggiano, 1½ teaspoons of the salt, and the egg and then give the mixture a few light stirs with a wooden spoon. Stir in the flours and combine until the mixture is sticky but releases from your hand when you press it (add more flour if needed). You want to blend the mixture without smashing it all together—more like fluffing it than mashing it. Make sure you scoop the potato and flour from the bottom of the bowl so you don't have any dry spots—you want it to look kind of like undermixed pie dough.

recipe continues

4 Lightly flour your work surface and place the dough on top. Divide the dough into four equal pieces and shape each into a ¾"-thick rope. Use a bench knife or chef's knife to slice the rope on a sharp bias in about ½" to ¾" intervals. Lightly dust a rimmed sheet pan with semolina and transfer the gnocchi to the baking sheet. Lightly sprinkle the top of the gnocchi with more semolina (so they don't stick together). Repeat with the other three pieces of dough (you'll end up with 80 to 90 pieces).

5 Spread some of the pomodoro sauce (or marinara sauce) across the bottom of a shallow serving platter or individual bowls. Bring a large pot of water to a boil. Add the remaining 2 tablespoons of salt and about 15 pieces of gnocchi (you don't want to crowd the pot). After a few minutes the gnocchi will float to the top. Let them bob around at the top of the simmering water until they are cooked through (you may have to sacrifice one and slice through it to make sure), about 2 minutes (they should collect together at the surface and stay there without sinking and rising again). Use a slotted spoon to transfer them to the sauced platter or bowls. Continue to cook the remaining gnocchi, then finish them with the rest of the sauce, some grated Parmigiano-Reggiano, and a few small basil leaves.

Make–Ahead Gnocchi

I often like to make a double batch of gnocchi because it's really just as easy as making a single batch. After the gnocchi rise to the surface of the boiling water, instead of letting them cook through, quickly transfer them to a large plate to cool. Drizzle the par-cooked gnocchi with a little olive oil (to prevent sticking) and transfer to a resealable freezer bag. The gnocchi will keep in the freezer for up to 3 months. To serve, simply plunge the frozen gnocchi into boiling water for 1 minute, then serve with a pomodoro sauce like the one on page 145, or pan-fry in a skillet, as in the Pan-Fried Sweet Potato Gnocchi recipe on page 152.

FLOUR 101

Just like you may use a different kind of sweetener to bake a cake (molasses versus brown sugar versus honey versus powdered sugar . . . and the list goes on), you can choose a specific flour that will more or less suit the desired texture of what you are cooking or baking.

Cake Flour: This is a low-protein flour often used for (you guessed it) cake or tender pastries that need less structure than, say, a loaf of sourdough bread.

00 Flour (Doppio Zero): A very soft low-protein, fine flour used for making supple and smooth doughs, like for pasta and pizza.

Pastry Flour: This flour provides more protein and structure than cake flour does, yet it's not quite as strong as all-purpose flour. Great for biscuits, scones, and pie crusts. For some reason, white pastry flour can be hard to find, so when I need an in-between flour, I'll often use half cake flour and half all-purpose (as in the Potato-Ricotta Gnocchi recipe on page 149).

All-Purpose Flour: A versatile medium-protein flour that can be used for most anything.

Bread Flour: A high-protein flour that is meant for high-heat mixing and kneading. This flour can handle the intense manipulation required for homemade breads.

PAN-FRIED SWEET POTATO GNOCCHI *Serves 8*

Gnocchi

2 medium sweet potatoes (preferably white Japanese sweet potatoes)

1 cup whole-milk ricotta

¼ cup finely chopped chives

2 teaspoons plus 1 tablespoon fine sea salt

½ teaspoon freshly ground black pepper

1 cup all-purpose flour, plus extra for shaping

Garlic Butter and Serving

6 tablespoons unsalted butter

¼ cup canola or grapeseed oil

4 medium garlic cloves, very thinly sliced

⅔ cup finely grated Parmigiano-Reggiano cheese

According to my team at the atelier, I get a real energy burst from potatoes—like a *crazy* energy burst. So I usually save my potato indulgences for when I am entertaining, which is probably why I just love making gnocchi for company. I get to indulge while feeding my guests something delicious and handmade. White sweet potatoes, sometimes called Japanese sweet potatoes, can be found in the late fall through winter in farmers' markets and some health food stores. I find them perfect for gnocchi because they add just enough sweetness without being *too* sweet like a standard orange sweet potato or yam can be. I make the gnocchi more or less the same way I make regular potato gnocchi, except for one key additional step: After poaching the dumplings in simmering water, I immediately brown them in garlic butter until they are crispy on both sides, then serve them under a blizzard of grated Parmigiano-Reggiano cheese. Talk about sinful! I also love them with applesauce on the side—see page 173 for a great sugar-free version.

1 *To make the gnocchi:* Place the potatoes in a medium saucepan and cover with water. Bring the water to a boil over high heat, reduce the heat to a simmer, and cook the potatoes until a paring knife easily slips into the center without meeting any resistance, 30 to 35 minutes, depending on how large the potatoes are. Drain the potatoes and, once they are cool enough to handle, peel away the skin. (I like to save it for snacking.)

2 Cut the potatoes into quarters and push them through a potato ricer (or food mill) and into a medium bowl. Add the ricotta, chives, 2 teaspoons of the salt, and the pepper and use a wooden spoon to stir to combine. Add the flour and stir to combine until the mixture is sticky but releases from your hand when you press it (add more flour if needed).

3 Divide the dough into four equal pieces. Heavily sprinkle your work surface with flour and place one piece of dough on top. Knead the dough into a thick rectangle shape and then roll it to a ½"-thick rope that is of even width from end to end. Use a knife or bench knife to cut the gnocchi on a diagonal into ½"-thick pieces and scoot them aside, covering them with a clean kitchen towel. Repeat with the remaining dough and using more flour as needed.

4 *To make the garlic butter:* Heat the oven to 250°F. Melt the butter in a large nonstick skillet over medium heat. Add the canola or grapeseed oil and garlic and reduce the heat to low, letting the garlic gently brown (if the garlic gets too brown, turn off the heat and turn it back on just before adding the first round of gnocchi).

5 Bring a large saucepan of water to a boil over high heat. Add the remaining 1 tablespoon of salt and reduce the heat to medium, then add about 10 pieces of gnocchi—enough to fill the saucepan without crowding the gnocchi (you don't want them to stick together). Let the gnocchi rise to the surface— this takes about 2 minutes. Once they rise to the surface, let them cook for 1 additional minute and then use a slotted spoon to transfer them to the hot garlic butter and brown on both sides, 2 to 3 minutes total. While the gnocchi browns in the garlic butter, poach more raw gnocchi. Use a slotted spoon to transfer the fried gnocchi to a rimmed sheet pan lined with parchment paper and place them in the warm oven. Repeat until all of the gnocchi are fried.

6 Transfer the gnocchi to a serving platter and sprinkle with the Parmigiano-Reggiano. Divide into bowls and serve hot.

HERB-ROASTED CHICKEN OVER VEGETABLES WITH BROWNED BUTTER GRAVY *Serves 4*

Roasted Chicken

1 chicken
(3½–4 pounds)

4 tablespoons unsalted butter, at room temperature

1 tablespoon curry powder

1 large leek, tough green top and root end removed

1 small yellow onion, quartered (or 3 medium cipollini onions, peeled and halved)

1 large or 2 medium parsnips, quartered lengthwise and sliced on a diagonal into ¾" pieces

1 large fennel bulb, quartered lengthwise, cored, and sliced lengthwise into thin pieces

½ pound butternut squash, seeded, peeled, and cut into 1" pieces

6 large garlic cloves, 3 smashed with the side of a knife

¼ cup extra-virgin olive oil

3 teaspoons coarse sea salt, plus extra to taste

For years I have experimented with what I think is *the perfect* dinner party meal, and here it is: a gorgeous, juicy roasted chicken with beautiful big-flavored and tender-roasted vegetables and a silky gravy to dress everything up. Guests always ask me how I get my chicken to be so moist and flavorful. Well, there are two tricks: Let the chicken sit out at room temperature before cooking so the breast meat is done at the same time as the legs (goodbye to dry white meat), and massage it with a spiced butter. I like adding curry powder to the butter as it infuses the chicken with a soft flavor and gives the skin a beautiful golden glow, without making the chicken taste too heavily spiced. The flavor becomes soft and warm because it is tempered by the essence of the fresh bundles of herbs, garlic, lemon, and cinnamon stick that I stuff inside the chicken. For a vegetarian option, roast some of the vegetables separately in a smaller baking dish.

---

1 *To make the chicken:* Rinse the outside and inside of the chicken under cool running water. Set it on a cutting board and use paper towels to pat the inside and outside very dry. Place the chicken on a plate and set it aside at room temperature to rest for at least 30 minutes or up to 1 hour. In a small bowl, stir together the butter and curry powder until it is smooth.

2 Preheat the oven to 425°F. Line a 3-quart casserole dish or a deep roasting pan with aluminum foil. Slice the leek in half lengthwise, remove the tough outer layer (save it for stock), and run the leek under cold running water to dislodge any dirt or sediment that might be trapped between the layers. Slice it on a diagonal into ¾"-wide pieces. Add the leek to a large bowl

recipe continues

1½ teaspoons freshly ground mixed peppercorns

1 bunch fresh thyme

1 lemon, ends removed

¼ cup store-bought or homemade chicken broth (page 208)

3 sprigs fresh rosemary

2 sprigs fresh sage

1 cinnamon stick

Gravy
1 tablespoon unsalted butter

1 tablespoon all-purpose flour

Reserved chicken jus (from the roasted chicken)

¼ cup chicken broth (if needed)

¼ teaspoon coarse sea salt, plus extra to taste

¼ teaspoon freshly ground mixed peppercorns

¼ teaspoon very finely chopped fresh rosemary

along with the onion, parsnip, fennel, squash, and smashed garlic. Add the olive oil, 1 teaspoon of the salt, and ½ teaspoon of the pepper and toss to combine.

3 Transfer the vegetables to the prepared dish or pan. Strip the leaves off of two sprigs of thyme (take from the bunch) and sprinkle the thyme over the vegetables. Roll the lemon on a cutting board to soften the interior membranes (this helps the juices flow more easily), then use a chef's knife to slash the skin of the lemon all over (this will encourage more of the essential oils to be released). Halve the lemon and slice one half into quarters. Nestle the quarters into the vegetables (set the other half aside). Add the chicken broth.

4 Place the chicken on the cutting board and liberally season the inside and outside of the chicken with the remaining 2 teaspoons of salt and remaining 1 teaspoon of pepper. Rub the chicken with the butter-curry mixture, making sure to get under the wings and legs and to evenly coat the top and back.

5 Stuff the chicken with the rosemary, sage, the remaining thyme, the remaining garlic, and the cinnamon stick. Hold the reserved lemon half over the cavity stuffed with herbs, gently give it a squeeze, and then tuck it in. Use twine or aluminum foil to tie the base of the legs together.

6 Set the chicken on top of the vegetables and sprinkle with a few pinches of salt. Roast until an instant-read thermometer inserted into the thigh joint reads 165°F, about 45 minutes (if you slit the skin and the thigh joint, the juices should run clear). Remove the pan from the oven and transfer the chicken to a large plate (it will rest while you finish the vegetables and gravy). Turn off the oven.

7 Use a metal spoon to gently push the vegetables over to one side and drain all of the pan juices into a medium bowl. Spread the vegetables in an even layer and return them to the oven to keep warm. Carefully untie the chicken legs and remove and discard the lemon, herbs, and cinnamon stick from the cavity. Tip the chicken over the bowl—quite a bit of jus should come out—reserve this for the gravy. Spoon off some of the fat that rises to the top and discard.

8 *To make the gravy:* Melt the butter in a medium saucepan over medium heat. Cook until it becomes browned and smells nutty, 3 to 4 minutes. Sprinkle in the flour, turn off the heat, and use a wooden spoon to stir the flour into the butter to create a paste (the flour can burn quickly, which is why I like to turn off the heat). Set the heat on medium-low and whisk in the warm chicken jus a little at a time so you don't get lumps. If, after adding the jus, the gravy is too thick, add some (or all) of the chicken broth. Continue to gently simmer for 2 minutes to cook out the raw flour taste. Stir in the salt, pepper, and rosemary. Taste and add more salt, if needed. Pour the gravy into a gravy boat.

9 Serve the chicken whole or carved and surrounded by the vegetables with the gravy on the side.

The Power of Smell

Just as I have to take my hand to fabric to feel how it moves and understand how it will drape, a cook always smells his or her ingredients before using them in a dish. I like to close my eyes and imagine how everything will taste together—the herbs, the spices, the citrus, the oil. Remember that, like perfume, scents change with the application of heat. It's something to keep in mind when choosing the quantity of herbs and spices (fresh herbs often become more muted when cooked, and spices tend to get stronger). When it comes to experimenting, I highly recommend not waiting until company comes over. Try your ideas out on yourself or a small group of close friends who are coming over, and save the tried-and-true creations for occasions when you want everything to be spot-on perfect.

HEIDI IS COMING TO DINNER!

Every summer, my *Project Runway* team reunites for a few crazy weeks of long shoots sprinkled with lots of laughs. We're like a family at this point—I guess that's what happens when you spend so many hours a day with the same cast and crew members. I first met my co-judge and host Heidi Klum when I cast her in one of my fashion shows back in 2003. Since then, Heidi, the model, has become a major superstar. She's a businesswoman who just doesn't stop, somehow balancing her devotion to her four children with her global enterprises and multiple television shows. Heidi is a beautiful force and friend!

One day during a break from shooting, Heidi told me she wanted to come over to my house for dinner. And I didn't even have to obsess about choosing a menu because she did that for me based on my Instagram photos. She even chose alternate options just in case. Heidi proposed a three-course dinner *plus* dessert, and of course I didn't want to disappoint, so off I went into an intense afternoon of cooking. I had the most fun preparing a really lovely meal for our intimate dinner party. I planned the meal for 8:00 in the evening, but I didn't realize that she was performing at Radio City Music Hall that evening and was coming over afterward. So she didn't get to my place until 10:30 that night! I made a simple puréed vegetable soup that's elegant and easy to re-warm, plus a roasted chicken with vegetables and gravy, which is so comforting yet chic, and is also great warm or at room temperature (meaning dinner can revolve around your needs rather than the demands of a dish). Add a simple fresh salad, a fresh sorbet for dessert, and there you have it: a late-night dinner fit for a model, business mogul, and TV star.

"Comforting yet chic."

A DINNER PARTY FOR HEIDI

Spring Watercress Soup *(page 6)*

Herb-Roasted Chicken over Vegetables with Browned Butter Gravy *(page 157)*

Mizuna and Avocado Salad with Creamy Cashew-Ginger Dressing *(page 83)*

Minty Melon Ice *(page 126)*

LATE FALL ROASTED RATATOUILLE *Serves 4*

8 ounces marble potatoes, halved

5 medium tomatoes, cored and sliced into wedges

4 medium garlic cloves, roughly chopped

2 medium beets, cut into ¾" pieces

2 medium carrots, peeled and sliced ½" thick on a diagonal

2 ribs celery, sliced ½" thick on a diagonal

1 red bell pepper, halved, seeded, and sliced into ½"-thick strips

1 medium leek, sliced ½" thick on a diagonal

1 medium Japanese eggplant, cut into ¾" pieces

1 medium zucchini, sliced ½" thick on a diagonal

3 fresh bay leaves (or 1 dried bay leaf)

1 sprig fresh rosemary, leaves removed

2 tablespoons roughly chopped fresh flat-leaf parsley

3 tablespoons extra-virgin olive oil

2 teaspoons sea salt

1 teaspoon finely chopped fresh thyme leaves

½ teaspoon freshly ground black pepper

Most recently, I transformed a tennis court at the country house into a garden by constructing raised beds on the court. The court was already surrounded by a high fence— perfect for protecting the garden from deer and other four-legged thieves! We planted tons of tomatoes and peppers, lots of herbs (including lemongrass!), Swiss chard, Brussels sprouts . . . you name it. This ratatouille was inspired by a late-fall harvest of random vegetables and herbs. I just put every-thing on a sheet pan and roasted it together, and it became this most delicious and flavorful fall ratatouille. It's delicious on its own, as a side dish to a roast, or tossed with pasta.

1 Preheat the oven to 350°F. Add the potatoes, tomatoes, gar-lic, beets, carrots, celery, bell pepper, leek, eggplant, zucchini, bay leaves, rosemary, parsley, olive oil, salt, thyme, and black pepper to a large bowl and toss to combine. Turn the mixture out onto a rimmed sheet pan and roast for 45 minutes.

2 Stir the vegetables and continue to roast until slightly browned and juicy, 35 to 45 minutes longer. Taste and adjust with more salt or black pepper if needed.

3 Remove and discard the bay leaves. Transfer the ratatouille to a bowl and serve warm or at room temperature.

Sharing the Bounty

Before I head back to the city to begin my workweek, I go out to the garden and harvest as many vegetables as I can to share with everyone in the atelier. Sharing the wealth of the garden is one of the great pleasures of my life. Besides the freshness that it brings to my cooking, I stand amazed by the physical forms that the differ-ent flowers and vegetables take—some elongate, some twist, some show off the most amazing and unexpected colors. I am sure that having these wonderful vegetables in the office provides inspiration when I am designing. Mother Nature really is the best couturier that I have ever encountered!

CRISPY CHICKEN FINGERS WITH ROASTED PEPPER AIOLI

Serves 4

Chicken Fingers

1 cup chickpea flour

3 tablespoons potato flour

1½ teaspoons baking powder

½ teaspoon fine sea salt

1 tablespoon honey

1 tablespoon mirin rice wine

1 tablespoon soy sauce

1½ pounds boneless, skinless chicken breasts

2 cups panko bread crumbs (gluten-free if you prefer)

Canola or vegetable oil, for frying (about 6 cups)

Roasted Pepper Aioli

1 roasted red bell pepper (homemade, see box on next page, or store-bought), very finely chopped

2 tablespoons Dijon mustard

2 tablespoons apple cider vinegar

1 tablespoon sambal oelek

1 tablespoon honey

1 teaspoon fine sea salt

½ cup extra-virgin olive oil

It is my goal to make everyone feel happy and tended to when I cook. I'll often fry up this sure-bet pleaser for kids. Instead of coating the chicken in a straight flour batter, I use chickpea flour for extra nutrition and panko bread crumbs for crunch. The dipping sauce is sweet-sour and just a touch spicy. It's a sneaky way to add flavors like sambal oelek, an Indonesian chile garlic sauce, and the naturally earthy flavor of chickpea flour. Introducing new flavors via a familiar package is a great way to get kids to expand their culinary horizons!

---

1 *To make the chicken fingers:* Whisk together the chickpea flour, potato flour, baking powder, and salt in a medium bowl. Combine the honey, mirin, and soy sauce with 1 cup of warm water in another bowl and stir to dissolve. Pour the liquid over the dry ingredients and whisk until the batter is completely smooth. Set the batter aside to rest for 30 minutes.

2 Place the chicken breasts on a cutting board and slice them on a bias into 1"-wide strips. Add the chicken to the batter, stirring to completely coat all sides of each piece. Place the bread crumbs in a separate bowl.

3 Pour enough canola or vegetable oil into a large saucepan to fill it to a 3" depth. Heat the oil over high heat until it comes to 350°F. Line a large plate with paper towels and set it near the saucepan. Take a piece of chicken and let the batter drip off, then roll it in the bread crumbs. Carefully place the chicken into the hot oil. Repeat with a few more pieces of chicken (don't overcrowd the pan; otherwise, the temperature of the oil will drop, resulting in soggy chicken fingers!) and fry on all sides until the chicken coating is deeply golden brown, 5 to 6 minutes, using a slotted spoon or frying spider to turn the chicken often (if you're unsure whether or not the chicken finger is cooked through, remove it from the oil and press on it—it should give slightly to semi-firm pressure—or cut into it to make sure the meat is opaque yet juicy). Transfer the chicken to the paper towel–lined plate to drain, then repeat with the remaining pieces.

4 *To make the roasted pepper aioli:* Meanwhile, add the roasted bell pepper, mustard, vinegar, sambal oelek, honey, and salt to a medium bowl and whisk until well combined. Slowly drizzle in the olive oil a little at a time (if the oil is added too quickly, the sauce can separate) to create a thick and creamy sauce. Once all of the oil is added, taste the sauce and adjust the flavor with more salt if needed. Serve the chicken fingers with the sauce on the side.

Roasting Peppers

Adjust an oven rack to the upper-middle position and heat the broiler to high. Place the pepper on a rimmed sheet pan and broil until all sides are charred, using tongs to turn the pepper every 6 to 8 minutes. Remove the pepper from the oven and place it in a heat-safe bowl. Cover the bowl with plastic wrap and set aside until the pepper is cool enough to handle, about 15 minutes. Pull the stem off the pepper and turn it upside down to drain off the liquid. Peel the blackened skin off the pepper, then open the pepper and remove the seeds. Do not rinse the pepper under water or you'll wash away the flavor! And don't rub your eyes! Set the peeled pepper aside to use as the recipe directs.

4 tablespoons unsalted butter

1 tablespoon extra-virgin olive oil

8 ounces brown mushrooms, stemmed and quartered

1 small sweet potato or 1 small Yukon gold potato, peeled and cut into ½" pieces

1 large carrot, peeled and cut into ½" pieces

1 rib celery, finely chopped

1 medium red or yellow onion, finely chopped

1 medium parsnip or turnip, peeled and cut into ½" pieces

1 small leek, white and light green parts only, thinly sliced

1 small apple, halved, cored, peeled, and finely chopped

5 garlic cloves, minced

5 fresh sage leaves, finely chopped

2 teaspoons finely chopped fresh thyme or 1 teaspoon dried

1 teaspoon finely chopped fresh rosemary

2½ teaspoons sea salt

1 teaspoon freshly ground black pepper

1 dried bay leaf

¼ cup all-purpose flour

1 sheet store-bought all-butter puff pastry dough (or 2 sheets if making individual pot pies)

⅓ cup finely grated Parmigiano-Reggiano cheese (optional)

VEGGIE POT PIE

Makes one 9½" deep-dish pot pie or 6 individual pot pies (using 6-ounce ramekins)

Pot pie seems to be a favorite dish served at fashion events in New York City. Sometimes it's made with chicken and sometimes lobster, and it's always hearty and comforting. It's amusing that pot pie has become a fashion world favorite . . . like a little black dress, always in style! I like making mine with lots and lots of hearty and healthy vegetables—whatever I can find in season at the green market is usually what goes into the pot (pie).

1 Heat 1 tablespoon of the butter and the olive oil in a heavy-bottomed Dutch oven over medium-high heat. Once the butter is melted, add the mushrooms, sweet potato, carrot, celery, onion, parsnip, leek, apple, garlic, sage, thyme, rosemary, salt, and pepper. Cook, stirring often, until the vegetables begin to soften, about 10 minutes (stir often so they don't brown).

2 Preheat the oven to 425°F. Add enough water to the pot with the vegetables to just cover them. Add the bay leaf and bring to a boil over high heat. Reduce the heat to medium-low and gently simmer until the carrot and potato begin to soften but aren't fully cooked, 5 to 8 minutes.

3 While the vegetables soften in the water, make the roux: Melt the remaining 3 tablespoons of butter in a small skillet over medium heat. Continue to cook, swirling the butter often, until it turns nutty brown and is fragrant, 3 to 4 minutes. Stir in the flour until the mixture looks pasty and cook until it turns a rich brown color, 2 to 3 minutes. Use a ladle to add about ½ cup of the broth from the vegetable pot into the skillet, stirring vigorously to remove any lumps (the mixture will be very thick). Continue to add vegetable liquid until the roux is

recipe continues

the consistency of a thick cream soup (you'll use about 2 cups of the broth), 3 to 5 minutes.

4 Pour the roux mixture into the pot with the vegetables and cook together for 5 minutes. Discard the bay leaf. Turn off the heat and add the mixture to a 9½" pie plate or divide among 6 ramekins.

5 If using a pie plate and your pastry is rectangular or square shaped, cut it into a 10" circle (if the pastry is circle shaped, you don't need to do anything). If using ramekins, use an upturned glass or cookie cutter to stamp out circles that are a little bigger than the circumference of the ramekin. Prick the pastry with a fork all over, then lay it over the pie plate (or ramekins). Trim off the overhang pastry (you can save some and use it to make a design on top if you like). Cut a few steam holes in the top of the pastry.

6 Set the pie plate or ramekins on a rimmed sheet pan and bake until the crust begins to turn golden, about 15 minutes. Sprinkle the cheese over the top (if using) and continue to bake until the pastry is deep brown, about 10 minutes longer. Remove from the oven and cool for at least 10 minutes before serving.

CURRIED SWEET CORN

Serves 4

4 large ears corn, kernels sliced away (about 4 cups)

2 tablespoons unsalted butter, melted

1 tablespoon curry powder

1 teaspoon granulated sugar

½ teaspoon sea salt

¼ teaspoon freshly ground black pepper

¼ cup finely chopped fresh cilantro

I devised this method that counts on the broiler to quickly singe kernels of corn so they can go from market to table in less than 10 minutes. Serving severed kernels off the cob is a little more elegant and dinner table friendly compared to the casualness of corn on the cob. I toss kernels with melted butter and curry powder, one of my favorite spice blends, but if you're not a fan of the fenugreek-turmeric flavor, leave it out or use garam masala, another type of Indian spice blend that is more cumin-cinnamony than curry powder. Be sure to save the corncobs in a resealable plastic bag in the freezer to make vegetable broth or corn stock.

---

1 Adjust an oven rack to the top position and preheat the broiler to high. Add the corn to a medium bowl and toss with the butter, curry powder, sugar, salt, and pepper.

2 Turn the corn out onto a rimmed sheet pan and broil it until it starts to sizzle, 4 to 5 minutes. Give the pan a shake to redistribute the corn and continue to broil until the corn is lightly browned on top, 3 to 4 minutes longer.

3 Remove the sheet pan from the oven and transfer the corn to a serving bowl. Sprinkle with the cilantro and serve.

A RAINBOW OF LENTILS

Lentils come in a variety of colors and cook up with different textures depending on the type of lentil you're using. Here's a rundown:

Black Lentils (sometimes called Beluga lentils): Small black lentils that hold their shape beautifully and even resemble caviar!

White Lentils: The hulled black lentil (see above)—very mild in flavor.

Brown Lentils: These are the most common lentil found in grocery stores. They cook up with a very tender texture and purée nicely for soups.

Red Lentils: The most common type of lentil for making Indian dal, these are actually hulled brown lentils. They cook up very soft and don't hold their shape well, making them good for sauces and soups.

Yellow Lentils: Another type of lentil that cooks up very soft and doesn't hold its shape well. Great for soups and dal.

French Green (Puy) Lentils: A small lentil with a nice textural bite—they tend to stay more firm than brown lentils, making them an excellent choice for salads.

Storing Spices

I use a lot of spices in my cooking. Flavors from across the globe inspire me in countless ways and transport me to faraway places where I have yet to visit, or places that I long to return to. To keep my spices superfresh, I store ground spices for up to just 6 months in a cool, dark, and dry spot (not near the stove!). Whole spices stay fresh for up to 1 year—once they are ground, though, the essential oils are activated and their freshness is limited. Now, nothing bad will happen if you use old spices; it's just that their flavor and pungency will be diminished. It's best to buy spices from a spice shop or a market (like an Indian or Middle Eastern grocer) that goes through a lot of spices. Some jars of spices at the supermarket can be months and months old. Just look at the color of the spice inside and ask yourself—does it look vibrant and fresh? Bright and colorful? If not, leave the spice on the shelf and seek out somewhere else to spend your money!

SPICED LENTILS *Serves 4*

2 tablespoons vegetable oil

6 medium garlic cloves, minced

1 heaping tablespoon finely grated fresh gingerroot

1 tablespoon plus 1 teaspoon curry powder

1 teaspoon ground cumin

½ teaspoon ground sumac (optional; if not using, serve the lentils with a lime wedge)

½ teaspoon ground turmeric

¼–½ teaspoon cayenne pepper (depending how spicy you like your lentils)

1½ teaspoons fine sea salt, plus extra if needed

½ teaspoon freshly ground black pepper

1 cup canned chopped tomatoes

2 cups red lentils (masoor dal)

½ cup coconut milk or heavy cream

Finely chopped fresh cilantro, for serving

Lime wedges, for serving (if you used sumac, you don't need the lime)

I try to cook vegetarian food at least a few times a week, and lentils have the protein, fiber, and B vitamins to make them a mainstay in my roster of dishes. My mom makes a simple vinaigrette-dressed lentil salad from *The Silver Palate Cookbook* for parties on New Year's Day. What a great and healthy (as well as auspicious, since many believe lentils and beans bring good luck when served on the first of the year) start to a new year. Lentils are used in so many cuisines—I've eaten them in France, Morocco, Egypt, and India, and in each place they are prepared differently, yet they always share the attribute of amazing flavor. What makes this version special are the spices that will make your kitchen smell like a fantastic Moroccan spice market. You can buy ground sumac online or in Middle Eastern and Indian markets. These lentils are really extra special when paired with the Minty Quinoa on page 172.

1   Heat the vegetable oil in a large saucepan over medium-high heat. Add the garlic and ginger and cook until it becomes fragrant, about 30 seconds. Stir in the curry powder, cumin, sumac (if using), turmeric, cayenne pepper, salt, and black pepper.

2   Once the spices start to sizzle, stir in the tomatoes, lentils, and 4 cups of water. Bring the water to a boil over high heat, then reduce the heat to medium-low and gently simmer until the lentils break down and the dal becomes thick, 25 to 30 minutes. Stir in the coconut milk, taste, and add more salt if needed. Sprinkle with cilantro and serve with lime wedges (if you didn't use sumac).

PONZU BRUSSELS SPROUTS *Serves 4*

3 tablespoons extra-virgin olive oil

1 pound Brussels sprouts, ends trimmed and sprouts halved

3 tablespoons Japanese ponzu sauce

2 large garlic cloves, smashed

½ teaspoon sea salt

Along with kale and cauliflower, Brussels sprouts are part of the new "cool kid" vegetable crowd. If you think you don't like them, try them my way: Instead of going with tradition and steaming or boiling them, which can accentuate their cabbagey taste, I roast them to bring out their natural sweetness. I also give them a good toss in a sweet-salty-citrusy ponzu-garlic marinade. If you can't find Japanese ponzu sauce (available in Asian markets and most supermarkets with an international aisle as well as online), you can substitute balsamic vinegar and a squeeze of lime juice or orange juice to good effect.

1 Preheat the oven to 375°F. Use a little of the olive oil to grease a rimmed sheet pan.

2 Toss the Brussels sprouts with the remaining oil, 2 tablespoons of the ponzu sauce, the garlic, and the salt in a large bowl. Turn the Brussels sprouts out onto the sheet pan (don't wash the bowl), flipping them over so the cut side faces down. Roast the Brussels sprouts until they are browned, 12 to 15 minutes.

3 Remove the pan from the oven and use tongs or a spatula to flip the sprouts over. Continue cooking until they are tender, 10 to 15 minutes longer.

4 Return the Brussels sprouts to the bowl, add the remaining 1 tablespoon of ponzu sauce, and toss to combine. Taste and season with more salt if needed. Transfer to a serving bowl if desired.

MINTY QUINOA *Serves 4*

½ cup golden raisins

2 cups quinoa, rinsed well under cold water and drained

½ cup finely chopped fresh mint leaves

Quinoa can be served in place of rice in almost any circumstance. I love this version in particular with the Spiced Lentils on page 169. The raisins in the quinoa give it a nice sweetness that works well with Middle Eastern and Indian dishes or anything that is a little spicy. The mint adds gorgeous color and flavor. In fact, this is a great high-protein dish to serve with some roasted vegetables and chopped toasted nuts for lunch or a light dinner. Just about any herb works here—try it with cilantro, basil, dill, or chopped fennel fronds.

1 Add the raisins to a large saucepan with 3 cups of water and bring to a boil. Stir in the drained quinoa and return the water to a boil. Reduce the heat to medium-low, cover the pan, and cook until the quinoa is tender and fluffy and has uncoiled (it kind of looks like it's sprouting), 16 to 18 minutes.

2 Turn off the heat, uncover the pan, and let the quinoa sit in the pan for 5 minutes. Use a fork to stir in the mint. Serve warm or at room temperature.

THE PUREST APPLESAUCE *Makes about 2¼ cups*

3 Granny Smith apples
(or other tart apples),
halved, cored, peeled,
and finely chopped

2 softer-textured sweet
apples (like McIntosh
or Jonagold), halved,
cored, peeled, and
finely chopped

Small pinch of fine
sea salt

In America we think of applesauce as a childhood treat—something that gets packed in a lunch box or served after naptime. But in Europe, applesauce is often served with dumplings, braised beef, or pork chops. Its fresh flavor and natural acidity and tartness are a great counterpoint to heavy dishes. When I was living in London and studying fashion design at Central Saint Martins, Anita Pallenberg took me under her wing and asked me to model for a Bella Freud campaign at her home, where we reenacted scenes from her iconic film, *Performance*, in which she had co-starred with Mick Jagger. Just like Anita's recipe for applesauce, I don't add anything at all to this applesauce except for water, making this perhaps the purest applesauce in the world. It's really great with the Pan-Fried Sweet Potato Gnocchi on page 152.

1 Add the apples, salt, and ¾ cup of water to a medium saucepan over high heat. Bring the water to a strong simmer, stirring the apples occasionally.

2 Reduce the heat to medium-low and continue to cook, stirring the apples often until they are soft and take on a glossy look, about 8 minutes. Give the apples a few good stirs to break down the chunks even more. (For a finer texture, pass the applesauce through a food mill.)

3 Transfer to a dish and serve warm, at room temperature, or chilled.

FLAKIEST APPLE PIE

Makes one 9" pie

3 tablespoons unsalted butter, at room temperature

3 Granny Smith apples, halved, cored, peeled, and cut into ¾" pieces

½ cup light brown sugar

1 tablespoon cornstarch

Juice of ½ lemon

1 teaspoon ground cinnamon

⅛ teaspoon ground cloves

2 pinches of sea salt

All-purpose flour, for rolling the dough

2 sheets store-bought puff pastry dough

1 large egg

Coarse sanding sugar (or sugar in the raw/Demerara sugar), for sprinkling

Whipped cream or ice cream, for serving

Baking gives me as much pleasure as draping a gown. And pie making is really one of my favorite weekend activities. Just the action of placing the top crust on and decorating it brings to mind piecing together a garment, and watching it come out of the oven, all browned and golden and gorgeous, is so immensely satisfying! In this version of apple pie, I use store-bought puff pastry dough instead of pie dough (page 50) for the bottom and top crusts. Not only does it make apple pie a last-minute dinner party dessert possibility (since you don't have to make and chill pie dough), but puff pastry is ridiculously flaky and buttery, which works so nicely with the creamy-sweet apple filling. For an extra rich and flavorful filling, I use brown sugar instead of plain white sugar. To gild the lily further, dot the top of the apples with browned butter, instead of using plain butter (page 33).

1   Use 1 tablespoon of the butter to grease a 9" pie dish. Toss the apples, brown sugar, cornstarch, lemon juice, cinnamon, clove, and a pinch of salt together in a large bowl and set aside.

2   Lightly flour your work surface and place one sheet of puff pastry on top. Sprinkle the top with a little flour and lightly roll the pastry until it is about ⅛" thick. Pick the pastry up and transfer it to the bottom of the buttered pie dish. Place the pie dish in the refrigerator and chill for 20 minutes. Preheat the oven to 400°F.

3   Whisk the egg with a pinch of salt and 1 teaspoon of water in a small bowl and set aside. Lightly flour your work surface again and lightly roll the second sheet of puff pastry until it is about ⅛" thick. Use a knife to slice strips of dough. They don't need to be even—in fact, I like to slice some thick and some very thin (see the picture of the lattice top on page 48).

4 Use a fork to prick the bottom of the pie crust all over, then add the apples to the chilled crust. Cut the remaining 2 tablespoons of butter into little bits and dot the top of the apples with them. Use a pastry brush to moisten the edge of the crust with the egg wash, then lay a strip of dough over the top of the apples, pressing down on the edges of the strip to stick to the bottom edge of the crust. Now lay a second strip across the first strip. Lay a third strip parallel to the first strip. Repeat until you have a fun lattice pattern. Use a knife to cut away any excess overhang around the rim of the pan. Brush the top of the dough with more egg wash and sprinkle with coarse sugar.

5 Bake the pie for 10 minutes, then reduce the temperature to 375°F and continue to bake until the crust is golden brown, 25 to 30 minutes. Remove from the oven and cool at least 30 minutes before slicing and serving with whipped cream or ice cream.

PUMPKIN–RYE MUFFINS

Makes 1 dozen

Sunflower Streusel

¼ cup granulated sugar

2 tablespoons all-purpose flour

¾ teaspoon ground cinnamon

¼ cup roasted sunflower seeds

Muffins

1¼ cups all-purpose flour

½ cup rye flour

1 teaspoon ground cinnamon

½ teaspoon ground nutmeg (preferably freshly grated)

½ teaspoon ground ginger

1 teaspoon baking soda

¼ teaspoon baking powder

1 teaspoon fine sea salt

½ cup (1 stick) unsalted butter, at room temperature

½ cup granulated sugar

½ cup packed dark brown sugar

2 large eggs

1 can (15 ounces) pumpkin (not pie filling)

¾ cup roasted sunflower seeds

It's nice to feel like you're getting something healthy from a muffin. These are tasty but not too sweet, with seasonings that remind me of Thanksgiving. The rye flour and sunflower seeds add depth. Be sure to buy pumpkin purée and not pumpkin pie filling—otherwise your muffins will turn out way too sweet!

1   Preheat the oven to 350°F. Place a muffin liner in each cup of a muffin pan and set aside.

2   *To make the sunflower streusel:* Stir the granulated sugar, all-purpose flour, cinnamon, and sunflower seeds together in a medium bowl. Set aside.

3   *To make the muffins:* Sift together the all-purpose flour, rye flour, cinnamon, nutmeg, ginger, baking soda, baking powder, and salt in a medium bowl and set aside.

4   Add the butter to the bowl of a stand mixer fitted with the paddle attachment (or to a large bowl if using a hand mixer). Cream the butter on medium-high speed until it is light and airy, about 30 seconds. Reduce the speed to medium and add the granulated and brown sugars. Increase the speed to medium-high and continue to beat until the mixture is airy, about 2 minutes.

5   Add the eggs one at a time, mixing well between additions. Add the pumpkin and beat until well combined. Remove the mixer bowl from the mixer.

6   Add the flour mixture in thirds, using a rubber spatula to fold it into the batter. Make sure just a few flour streaks remain before adding the next addition, and take care not to overmix. Stir in the sunflower seeds and then portion the batter into the muffin cups. Sprinkle some streusel over each muffin.

7   Bake until the center of a muffin resists light pressure and a cake tester inserted into the center comes out clean, 22 to 26 minutes. Cool in the pan for 15 minutes, then remove the muffins from the pan and serve warm or cool completely on a wire rack.

PISTACHIO CARROT CAKE WITH DULCE DE LECHE FROSTING *Serves 12*

Carrot Cake

1 cup (2 sticks) plus
1 tablespoon unsalted
butter, at room
temperature

1 cup shelled unsalted
pistachios

1 pound carrots
(about 5 large)

3 cups all-purpose
flour

2 teaspoons baking
powder

1 teaspoon baking
soda

1 teaspoon ground
cinnamon

1 teaspoon ground
ginger

½ teaspoon ground
cardamom

¼ teaspoon ground
cloves

1 teaspoon fine sea salt

1 cup granulated sugar

1 cup packed dark
brown sugar

¼ cup molasses

4 large eggs

Finely grated zest of
1 lemon, plus
2 tablespoons fresh
lemon juice

1½ teaspoons vanilla
extract

½ cup dried apricots,
finely chopped

¼ cup vegetable oil

ingredients continue

If you love carrot cake, if you crave carrot cake, make this carrot cake. It's moist, it's sweet, it's rich, it's decadent—it actually reminds me of a lovely English steamed "pudding" (and is so good served with clotted cream if you don't want to make the frosting!). Molasses, brown sugar, apricots, and a pound of carrots seal in moisture, making this cake as delicious on day 5 as it is on day 1 (if it even lasts that long . . . which is doubtful!). The caramel flavor of the dulce de leche and fresh ginger in the cream cheese frosting really send the flavor straight through the roof.

---

1 *To make the carrot cake:* Preheat the oven to 325°F. Grease a 10" tube pan with 1 tablespoon of the soft butter and wrap the bottom of the pan in a double layer of aluminum foil. Set the pan aside.

2 Add the pistachios to the bowl of a food processor fitted with a metal blade and pulse until finely chopped. Transfer the nuts to a medium bowl. Remove the blade from the food processor and replace it with the grater attachment (if you don't have a grater attachment, use the medium-hole side of a box grater instead), then grate the carrots and transfer them to a separate bowl.

3 Whisk together the flour, baking powder, baking soda, cinnamon, ginger, cardamom, cloves, and salt in a large bowl. Set aside.

4 Add the remaining 1 cup of butter to the bowl of a stand mixer fitted with the paddle attachment (or a large bowl if using a hand mixer). Cream the butter on medium-high speed until it is light and airy, about 1 minute. Reduce the speed to medium-low and add the granulated sugar, brown sugar, and molasses. Increase the speed to medium-high and beat until the mixture is airy, about 2 minutes. Scrape down the sides and bottom of the bowl as needed.

recipe continues

Dulce de Leche Frosting

8 ounces cream cheese, at room temperature

½ cup dulce de leche (see box, below)

½ cup sifted powdered sugar

1 teaspoon grated fresh gingerroot

1 tablespoon unsalted butter, at room temperature

5 Add the eggs, one at a time, beating well on medium-high speed between each addition. Scrape the bottom and sides of the bowl and then add the lemon zest and juice and the vanilla and beat until combined. Turn off the mixer and add the flour mixture, the carrots, apricots, vegetable oil, and all but ¼ cup of the pistachios. Mix on low speed until most of the flour is combined, then increase the mixer speed to medium and mix until no dry patches remain. Scrape the bottom and sides of the bowl as needed.

6 Use a rubber spatula to transfer the batter to the tube pan and smooth out the top of the batter. Bake the cake until it resists light pressure and a cake tester comes out clean, 1¼ to 1½ hours. Set the pan on a wire rack for 15 minutes. Run a knife around the edges of the cake and turn it over onto a cake plate. Remove the pan and then the tube insert and set the cake aside to cool completely.

7 *To make the dulce de leche frosting:* While the cake cools, add the cream cheese to the bowl of a stand mixer fitted with the paddle attachment. Cream it on medium speed until it is smooth, then add the dulce de leche and continue to cream until well combined. Turn off the mixer and add the powdered sugar and ginger. Beat on low speed until combined. Add the butter and beat on medium-high speed until nice and creamy, about 20 seconds.

8 Frost the top of the cake with the dulce de leche frosting and sprinkle with the remaining ¼ cup of pistachios. Slice and serve.

Homemade Dulce de Leche

From-scratch dulce de leche is made by slowly cooking milk and sugar together for a very long time (7 to 8 hours!). Make the faster homemade version by placing a can of sweetened condensed milk (peel off the label) in a deep pot and covering it with water. Bring the water to a simmer and gently cook the condensed milk in the can for 3 hours; if the water gets low, be sure to replenish it so the can is always covered. Remove the can from the pot and cool it completely before opening the can.

POACHED PEARS WITH MASCARPONE CREAM

Serves 8

2½ cups fruity white wine (such as a Riesling or Viognier)

1⅓ cups granulated sugar

1 star anise pod

4 Bosc pears, halved, cored, peeled, and center fibrous vein removed with a knife (keep the stem on)

1 cup heavy cream

2 tablespoons liqueur, such as pear brandy, Amaretto, or port (optional)

¼ teaspoon almond extract

1 cup mascarpone cheese

We have two pear trees at my family's farm in Pennsylvania, and dozens of pears always seem to ripen at the same moment in the late summer and early fall. The trick is to check on the trees every day so that you catch the pears at peak ripeness before they fall off the tree. One of my favorite ways to use up all of the pears is to poach them, because poached pears are so elegant on their own. They can also be turned into a myriad of dessert (and even savory) options. I'll often bring in baskets of pears to the atelier to share with my team, who are always so excited to get fresh produce and fruit from the country.

1 Add the wine, 1 cup of the sugar, and the star anise to a large pot. Add the pear halves and then add enough water so they are completely submerged, 1½ to 2 cups.

2 Bring the liquid to a soft simmer over medium-high heat, then reduce the heat to medium-low, cover the pot, and gently poach the pears until a paring knife easily slides into the center of one half without any resistance, 25 to 30 minutes. Uncover the pot and let the pears cool in the poaching liquid (if you're not serving within a few hours, refrigerate the pear halves in the poaching liquid for up to 1 week).

3 Add the cream, remaining ⅓ cup of sugar, the liqueur (if using), and almond extract to the bowl of a stand mixer fitted with the whisk attachment (or to a large bowl if whisking by hand or using a hand mixer). Whip on medium-high speed until the cream makes soft peaks. Add the mascarpone cheese and continue to whip on medium-high speed until the mixture is well combined and creamy.

4 Add a large dollop of the mascarpone cream to each dessert bowl. Lean a pear half on it and drizzle with poaching liquid.

IDEAS FOR USING POACHED PEARS AND POACHING LIQUID

There are so many ways to use poached pears—here are some of my favorites. And don't you dare pour any of the poaching liquid down the drain! Try one of the following delicious ways to make use of it.

USES FOR POACHED PEARS

- For breakfast with yogurt and granola
- Chop and add to muffins or quick bread batter
- Purée for pear sauce (instead of applesauce) and freeze in an ice cream maker to make sorbet
- Add to vanilla ice cream with caramel sauce and toasted nuts for a pear sundae
- Top a tart (page 242)
- Thinly slice and place over a cream pie or between frosting and cake layers
- Chop and add to sautéed onions, chile peppers, and Indian spices for chutney

USES FOR POACHING LIQUID

- Warm with cider and add a slug of rum for a wonderful warm pear punch (serve with a cinnamon stick!)
- Sweetening herbal tea
- Sweetening your favorite cocktail instead of using simple syrup
- Reduced over medium heat until it is thick and syrupy and poured over pancakes, waffles, or ice cream
- Dab over cake layers before frosting to add extra moistness
- Whisk with a little mustard and canola oil for a pear-infused salad dressing
- Pour it into a glass pan and freeze, raking with a fork every 20 minutes to make granita
- Blend with ice cubes and dessert wine for a gorgeous pear-wine ice

HOT CHOCOLATE BUNDT CAKE WITH GANACHE GLAZE *Serves 12*

Bundt Cake

1 cup (2 sticks) plus 2 tablespoons room temperature unsalted butter

2¼ cups all-purpose flour

1 cup best-quality hot cocoa mix

1 teaspoon baking soda

1 teaspoon fine sea salt

½ cup whole milk

½ cup sour cream

1 teaspoon vanilla extract

1 cup granulated sugar

½ cup packed light brown sugar

4 large eggs

¾ cup semisweet chocolate chips

Ganache Glaze

½ cup heavy cream

½ cup semisweet chocolate chips

½ tablespoon cold unsalted butter

My favorite place in the entire world for *chocolat chaud* (hot chocolate) is under an arcade in Paris near the Louvre. This is not a secret spot (Coco Chanel frequented it, too). Sometimes it seems as if nearly every tourist makes his or her way to Angelina's, and it never disappoints. The hot chocolate there is called *chocolat chaud l'Africain*. It is rich and thick and delicious. This was the inspiration for my Bundt cake recipe. When I pour the ganache glaze over the cake, I am transported to the magic of Paris.

---

1 *To make the Bundt cake:* Preheat the oven to 325°F. Use 2 tablespoons of the butter to heavily grease a 10½" (12- to 15-cup) Bundt pan. Whisk the flour, cocoa mix, baking soda, and salt together in a large bowl. Whisk the milk, sour cream, and vanilla together in a medium bowl.

2 Add the remaining 1 cup of butter, the granulated sugar, and brown sugar to the bowl of a stand mixer fitted with the paddle attachment (or a large bowl if using a hand mixer) and cream together on medium-high speed until very light and creamy, about 3 minutes, using a rubber spatula to scrape the bottom and sides of the bowl as needed. Reduce the speed to medium-low and add the eggs, one at a time, beating on medium-high speed between additions.

3 Reduce the speed to low and add one-third of the flour mixture. Once it is mostly incorporated, add half of the milk mixture. Add half of the remaining flour mixture followed by the remaining milk mixture and the rest of the flour. Increase the mixer speed to medium and beat until well combined, about 30 seconds. Stop the mixer and use a rubber spatula to scrape the bottom and sides of the bowl as needed.

recipe continues

4 Add half of the batter to the bottom of the buttered Bundt pan. Sprinkle the chocolate chips over the batter, then add the remaining batter over the chocolate chips, using a spatula to spread the batter out as evenly as possible. Bake the cake until a cake tester comes out with no wet cake batter on it (there may be melted chocolate, though, if you hit a chocolate chip), 50 minutes to 1 hour. Set the cake aside to cool completely, 2 to 3 hours.

5 *To make the ganache glaze:* Bring the cream to a simmer in a small saucepan over high heat. Add the chocolate chips to a medium bowl. Pour the hot cream over the chocolate, cover the bowl with a piece of plastic wrap, and set aside for 5 minutes. Remove the plastic wrap and whisk the cream and chocolate together until the mixture is thick and smooth. Whisk in the butter.

6 Turn the cake out onto a wire rack. Pour the glaze over the top of the cake and set it aside to set up. The cake is ready to slice and serve after 10 to 20 minutes, depending on how warm your kitchen is (and how quickly the ganache sets). Slice and serve.

MINT TEA *Makes 4 cups*

1 piece (2" long) fresh gingerroot, sliced ½" thick on a diagonal

¼ cup cane sugar

2 cups fresh mint

½ lemon, cut into wedges

My most vivid memories of mint tea come from a family trip to Morocco when I was 8 years old. Wherever we went, we were offered fresh mint tea. In fact, walking through winding alleyways of the medina in Fez, I could smell the mint and saw mules that were laden with masses of fresh mint. Moroccans believe that pouring the tea from about 3 feet above the glass cup enhances the flavor by aerating the tea—it's usually done to great dramatic effect, which I always appreciate. If I can get fresh mint (preferably from my garden), I love to brew it. My recipe riffs on traditional Moroccan mint tea slightly by adding fresh ginger.

1 Add 4½ cups of water to a small saucepan along with the ginger and bring to a boil over medium heat.

2 Add the sugar and stir until the sugar is dissolved. Turn off the heat, add the mint, and set aside for 5 minutes to steep.

3 Use a slotted spoon to remove the ginger and mint. Divide the hot tea into four mugs and serve each with a lemon wedge.

CAFFEINATED CHOCOLATE MOUSSE

Serves 6

8 ounces bittersweet chocolate, very finely chopped (about 1¼ cups)

2 cups heavy cream

6 tablespoons granulated sugar

3 large eggs plus 1 large egg yolk, at room temperature

3 tablespoons brewed espresso or very strong coffee

1 teaspoon vanilla extract

On special occasions when I was growing up, my parents took the family to fancy restaurants where, more often than not, chocolate mousse would be on the menu for dessert. I used to play a game where I would order chocolate mousse and then give it a rating, the criteria being texture (my favorite is firm but smooth, never soft or runny), the degree of sweetness (semisweet, of course), and temperature (not frozen!). There are so many variations when it comes to chocolate mousse—sometimes it is placed in a ramekin or a cup so it develops a skin on top (which some people like). Other times it is simply spooned out and formed into an oval-shaped torpedo called a quenelle. If you want something rich to end a meal, chocolate mousse is your dessert. You can make it in advance, which is fantastic for plan-ahead parties. I like to top mine with a little whipped cream and shaved dark chocolate—while a little sprig of mint always gives it that restauranty polished look.

1 Add 1" of water to a medium saucepan over medium-high heat. Once the water comes to a simmer, reduce the heat to low and place a heat-safe mixing bowl on top, making sure the bottom of the bowl doesn't touch the water (you can also use a double boiler if you have one). Add the chocolate to the bowl and stir every few minutes until the chocolate is melted. Remove the bowl from the saucepan and set aside.

2 Discard the water in the saucepan and add 1 cup of the cream to the saucepan with 2 tablespoons of the sugar and set it over medium heat. Stir the cream occasionally until the sugar is dissolved. Turn off the heat.

3 Separate the egg whites into the bowl of a stand mixer (or a large bowl if using a hand mixer) and set aside; add the four yolks to a medium bowl and whisk to combine. Pour a little of the hot cream into the bowl with the yolks and whisk to combine. Continue to slowly drizzle the cream in until all of the

cream is added (you do this slowly so the eggs don't scramble). Return the egg-cream mixture to the saucepan and set it over medium-low heat. Use a wooden spoon to stir slowly and constantly until the mixture thickens into a sauce (you will be able to draw a line in the back of the spoon that doesn't fill in immediately, and the sauce will start to thicken, especially in the corners of the pan), about 5 minutes.

4 Pour the egg-cream mixture through a fine-mesh sieve (to remove any lumps) and into the bowl with the chocolate. Whisk the chocolate with the egg-cream mixture to combine. Whisk in the espresso and set the mixture aside for 10 minutes to cool slightly.

5 Fit the stand mixer with the whip attachment and beat the egg whites until they hold stiff peaks (you'll be able to remove the whisk and the whites will be able to spike straight up without drooping). Add one-third of the whites to the chocolate mixture and whisk in, then add the remaining egg whites and use a whisk or rubber spatula to fold them in until just a streak or two of whites remain.

6 Clean the bowl of the stand mixer and the whisk. Add ½ cup of the remaining cream, 2 tablespoons of the remaining sugar, and the vanilla to the bowl and whip on medium-high speed until the cream holds stiff peaks. Whisk one-third of the whipped cream into the chocolate mixture, then add the rest and fold it in.

7 Transfer the mousse to six individual dessert cups or small bowls or to a 2-quart baking dish. Cover the cups or baking dish with plastic wrap and refrigerate for 8 hours or overnight to allow the mousse to set before serving. Whip the remaining ½ cup of cream with the remaining 2 tablespoons of sugar to medium peaks and serve the mousse either dolloped with whipped cream or with a bowl of whipped cream on the side.

HOLIDAY

The holidays represent a time when I can break away from my crazy life and spend time with my family and closest loved ones. I love planning the elaborate holiday meals, and especially love setting a beautiful and special table to signify the importance of the meal we are gathering to celebrate. There is Easter and Passover in the spring and the Fourth of July in the summer, but the fall and winter holidays are my favorites. There are so many lovely cooking traditions to explore and new ones to create—I find I do some of my best culinary experimentation from Thanksgiving through New Year's Day!

Thanksgiving seems to be the holiday that most directly ties to the change of seasons and the enjoyment of friends and family. My mornings often start with watching the Macy's Thanksgiving Day Parade on TV (I vividly recall being hoisted on my dad's shoulders in freezing weather to watch it live!), and then softly transitioning to spending the day in the kitchen and giving in to that wonderful feeling of being surrounded by the bustle of the meal coming together. My mom gets up before dawn to start the turkey; my aunt is passionately absorbed in making pies and desserts; and I am often in the dining room arranging the table and setting the tone. Every year I seem to end up participating more and more in the meal making. Being more involved in the preparation of the food is an honor that is passed down from one generation to the next.

The Thanksgiving that I remember best brought with it a food revelation. I learned about brining and massaging a turkey . . . when I was 6 years old. My parents had taken me to the Village Light Opera, where a friend, Patty Shay, was performing in an amateur Gilbert & Sullivan production of *Iolanthe*. Patty is also a professional chef, and she put my little hands to work to tenderize the bird, warning me not to break the skin because we were going to slide slices of pineapple under the turkey skin and secure them using cloves as tacks. Once the turkey finished roasting, it looked like something out of a banquet in a fairy tale. Bronzed, glistening, and so centerpiece-stunning. Thanksgiving dinner was served on a very long table made out of a magnificent slab of wood. The turkey was accompanied by a wild rice pilaf, stuffing cooked outside of the bird, and all the usual fixings, and I was included in not just the preparations but all the good conversations and fun of being at the grown-up table. Even now that I'm older, it's with a child's enthusiasm that I approach cooking for holidays every year. It's a special responsibility that I take seriously but also have fun with—I truly hope that never changes.

HOLIDAY

CARAMELIZED ONION CANAPÉS WITH CRÈME FRAÎCHE AND CAVIAR

Makes 40

1 tablespoon unsalted butter

1 tablespoon extra-virgin olive oil

3 large red onions, halved and thinly sliced

2 teaspoons finely chopped fresh thyme

¾ teaspoon plus a pinch of sea salt

1 large egg

All-purpose flour, for rolling the pastry

2 sheets store-bought puff pastry

¾ cup crème fraîche

2 tablespoons lemon juice

⅓ cup sevruga, osetra, or beluga caviar or whitefish roe or salmon roe

These hors d'oeuvres really impress. While the recipe makes 40, I bet you might want to double it depending on how many people you are entertaining (I've seen eight people easily go through an entire tray!). A respectable two or three per person is a good bet, in which case 40 serves 12 to 20 guests. If your wallet groans at the idea of caviar, you can substitute domestic whitefish roe or large glistening pearls of salmon roe, both of which are quite affordable.

1 Caramelize the onions: Add the butter and olive oil to a large skillet and heat over medium-high heat until the butter is melted, 1½ to 2 minutes. Add the onions and cook, stirring occasionally, until they are soft, about 15 minutes. Stir in the thyme, reduce the heat to medium-low, cover the pan, and continue to cook the onions until they are very dark purple and very soft and sticky, 35 to 45 minutes, stirring every 10 minutes or so. Stir in ½ teaspoon of the salt and set the onions aside.

2 Meanwhile, make the puff pastry bases: Preheat the oven to 400°F. Whisk the egg with a pinch of salt and 1 teaspoon of water in a small bowl. Lightly sprinkle your work surface with flour and set a piece of puff pastry on top. Roll the pastry until it is about ⅛" thick, then use a fork to dock the dough all over (so it doesn't puff up too much while baking). Use a small cookie cutter (I like using one that's about 2" in diameter, but use any size/shape you like) to stamp out pieces of pastry as closely together as possible so you don't waste too much of the dough.

3 Transfer the pastry to a rimmed sheet pan lined with parchment paper. Repeat with the remaining sheet of pastry dough

recipe continues

(you can crowd the pastry together—it doesn't spread). Lightly dab the tops of the dough pieces with the egg wash, then place a second piece of parchment paper on top of the dough and place a second sheet pan on top of the parchment to weigh down the cut-out pieces of pastry. (If you don't have a second sheet pan the same size, it's okay—just prick the pieces a few extra times to make sure they stay as flat as possible during baking.) Bake the pastry until it is golden brown and crisp, about 15 minutes. Remove from the oven and set aside to cool.

4 Whisk together the crème fraîche, lemon juice, and the remaining ¼ teaspoon of salt in a medium bowl. Place the baked and cooled pastry bottoms on a platter. Top a piece with a little of the onion mixture, then with a small spoonful of crème fraîche. Finish with about ½ teaspoon of caviar. Repeat with the remaining pastry bottoms and serve immediately. (The puff pastry bottoms can be stored in airtight containers for up to 3 days; the crème fraîche can be refrigerated for up to 3 days; and the caramelized onions can be refrigerated for up to 1 week.)

CINNAMON–SUGAR PECANS *Makes 4 cups*

2 tablespoons unsalted butter, at room temperature

½ cup granulated sugar

½ teaspoon ground cinnamon

½ teaspoon fine sea salt

1 large egg white

4 cups pecan halves (about 1 pound)

This recipe came to me from my Uncle Dan's mom. The pecans are sweet and salty, great as a snack or sprinkled over salad or yogurt and granola in the morning. This recipe is just as tasty made with peanuts or walnuts—or mix a few different nuts and pack in Mason jars as a gift.

1 Preheat the oven to 275°F. Use the butter to lightly grease a rimmed sheet pan and set aside.

2 Mix the sugar, cinnamon, and salt together in a small bowl and set aside.

3 Whisk together the egg white and 1 tablespoon of water in a medium bowl until the mixture is slightly frothy. Add the pecans and stir to coat. Add the sugar mixture, stirring to coat.

4 Transfer the pecans to the prepared pan and bake, stirring every 15 minutes, until the nuts are deeply toasty and glossy, about 1 hour total. Remove from the oven and set aside to cool, then transfer to a serving dish or airtight container (the nuts can be kept at room temperature for 1 week).

ROSEMARY SPICED PECANS *Makes 4 cups*

4 cups pecan halves (about 1 pound)

1½ tablespoons granulated sugar

2½ teaspoons ground cumin

1½ teaspoons fine sea salt

½ teaspoon freshly ground black pepper

¼ teaspoon cayenne pepper

¼ cup extra-virgin olive oil

2 tablespoons chopped fresh rosemary

Spiced nuts are easy to make ahead and store so that whenever you have drop-in holiday guests, you always have something tasty and homemade to offer them. Rosemary, cumin, and cayenne make a terrific combo that is piney, earthy, and spicy all at once. They're so simple to make that I'm offering a bonus sweet/spicy nut recipe (page 199) so you can have a variety of nuts in the house. I like to serve these in pretty decorative bowls alongside cocktails or on a buffet. Once the pecans come out of the oven and are cooled, you can store them in an airtight container at room temperature for a week.

1 Preheat the oven to 300°F. Line a rimmed sheet pan with parchment paper and set aside. Place the pecans in a medium heat-safe bowl and set aside. Stir the sugar, cumin, salt, black pepper, and cayenne together in a small bowl.

2 Add the olive oil to a small saucepan over medium-low heat. Add the rosemary and continue to warm the oil until it's fragrant, about 1 minute. Pour the oil over the pecans. Add the spice mixture to the pecans and toss to combine.

3 Transfer the pecans to the prepared sheet pan and spread out into an even layer. Bake, stirring the pecans every 8 minutes, until they are golden and fragrant, about 20 minutes. Remove from the oven and set aside to cool, then transfer to a serving dish or airtight container.

COOKING WITH THE GREATS
IN A LEGENDARY KITCHEN

It came as a surprise when, in 2009, the New York City Food and Wine Festival asked me if I would be interested in cooking at the James Beard House. I quickly said yes with great excitement. It was such an honor. James Beard was a great lover of food who penned a number of now iconic cookbooks. His home, a brownstone on West 12th Street (which I've walked past a million times throughout my life), has been turned into a nonprofit hub for dinners and events featuring the top chefs from around the country, many of whom are honored at the annual James Beard Awards, the Oscars of the cooking world. As a teenager, even before the Food Network, I voraciously watched a cooking show called *Great Chefs of the World* that focused on different master chefs preparing their signature dishes with a simple voiceover (a woman with a most lovely Southern drawl). I had seen episodes where meals were cooked in James Beard's kitchen, so I absolutely knew I had to accept the invitation to cook at the event!

My assignment was to prepare two courses of a meal for the 100-seat dining room. I'd be cooking alongside Marcus Samuelsson, the renowned chef of Swedish and Ethiopian heritage who had recently completely blown me away with his refined Swedish fusion fare (long before Nordic trendiness and the world-famous Noma took over the food scene) at Aquavit in New York City, and Giada De Laurentiis, who was already a food TV phenom. I arrived at about 11:30 a.m. to start prepping. It was the tiniest kitchen I could have imagined, and to think that it was going to be shared with two master chefs and their teams was daunting, to say the least!

After learning that Marcus and Giada were participating in the meal, I'd humbly and strategically decided to "keep it simple, stupid" and tackle an hors d'oeuvre and a soup, and leave the real deal meal to the pros. At about noon, Marcus's team showed up and started preparing chicken that would take all day to cook. They braised it and cooked it in aromatic curry seasonings that filled the tiny kitchen with a scent that reminded me of some mixture of Ethiopia and Mexico. I started my prep making roux for a spicy crawfish and fennel bisque. My "simple" idea quickly proved to be a nightmare—imagine shelling hundreds of crawfish in order to make a flavorful stock!

Then it was time to start preparing purple Peruvian potatoes to be filled with caviar, which the James Beard authorities insisted had to be domestic and farm-raised to meet their sustainability standards. I planned for the potatoes to be topped with a dollop of crème fraîche, green chives, and a little bluish-purple borage flower.

Giada soon arrived with her team and her own supply of homegrown basil. Both Marcus and Giada jumped into full prep as if they were on a military assignment. I had no team and was getting anxious. The tiny kitchen was starting to get claustrophobic with the three of us sharing the small amount of prep space. I think they could sense my angst because we quickly all decided to play as a team of chefs producing one dinner rather than three separate chefs creating separate courses. They would lend their hands and knowledge to my efforts, and I'd do the same (well, at least lend my hands!) to theirs. They laid the different ingredients that went into my hors d'oeuvres out on the prep table and showed me how to move quickly, as if on an assembly line.

Guests and press started to arrive, and the setup of the space required that everyone had to walk through the kitchen to get to the dining area. So not only did we have to cook fast, but we had to cook, clean, *and* look great *and* be up for chatting with the diners!

Time was ticking away. Marcus, Giada, and I went before the dining room and explained to the guests what was on the menu—me with my bisque and caviar-topped potatoes, Marcus with his chicken that he basted for hours with foie gras and pumpkin purée. He assured the crowd that the meat would fall off the bone delicately infused with his exotic herbs and blends; I was fascinated by how he managed not to dry out the chicken—a trick that still evades me. Giada presented her eggplant timbales and her chocolate truffle pops (who doesn't like chocolate?!). Giada and I collaborated on a poached pear and ginger ice cream dessert. The whole meal and collaboration was a huge success. To this day, I am so grateful for the support of Marcus and Giada. I was a fledgling in the kitchen, and they were kind and generous to me.

1 sprig fresh flat-leaf parsley, plus 2 tablespoons finely chopped for serving

1 sprig fresh rosemary

1 sprig fresh thyme

1 dried bay leaf

2 tablespoons unsalted butter or vegetable oil

1 large yellow onion, finely chopped

1 large shallot, halved and minced

2 teaspoons coarse sea salt, plus more to taste

6 shiitake mushrooms, stemmed and roughly chopped

1 medium carrot, peeled and finely chopped

1 medium rib celery, finely chopped

1 medium parsnip, peeled and finely chopped

½ teaspoon freshly ground black pepper

⅛ teaspoon ground cloves

⅛ teaspoon ground nutmeg (preferably freshly grated)

¼ cup dry white wine

4 cups store-bought or homemade chicken broth (page 208), plus more if needed

3 cups (1 pound) roasted and peeled chestnuts, roughly chopped

1 cup whole milk

½ cup heavy cream

½ cup crème fraîche, for serving (optional)

CHESTNUT SOUP *Serves 6*

I'm crazy about chestnuts. Their flavor is sweet and soft with a lilting floral and almost mushroomy note. Chestnuts purée into a very smooth cream that works terrifically in many desserts (page 247) as well as savories like this velvety, sultry soup. I grew up with a beautiful old chestnut tree that survived the chestnut blight that wiped out many of the American chestnut trees in the early 1900s. The tree was right outside my bedroom window at my parents' Bucks County farmhouse. I watched it flower in the spring with yellow blooms that resembled tiny firework bursts (great table decorations, by the way), followed by spiny spiky balls that would fall to the ground before they split open to reveal the shiny brown chestnuts inside. It was always a race to see who could gather the chestnuts first—me or the squirrels! If I could gather enough of them, I would roast them over a fire in our walk-in fireplace in the oldest part of the farmhouse, built around 1770. The soup is a lovely starter to a grander meal; I like serving it in vintage teacups with a dollop of crème fraîche and a drizzle of honey. For a dairy-free version, substitute neutral oil for the butter, use cashew milk instead of the milk and cream, and eliminate the crème fraîche.

1 Place the parsley sprig on a flat work surface and cover with the rosemary and thyme. Add the bay leaf and then use a piece of kitchen twine to tie the herbs together to make a small bundle. Set aside.

2 Melt the butter in a heavy-bottomed soup pot over medium-high heat. Add the onion, shallot, and 2 teaspoons of the salt, reduce the heat to medium, and cook, stirring often, until they are soft, about 5 minutes. Stir in the mushrooms, carrot, celery, and parsnip, reduce the heat to low, cover the pot, and cook, stirring occasionally, until the carrot is tender, 12 to 15 minutes (you can increase the heat if it seems like the vegetables aren't cooking, but take care not to brown them).

3 Uncover the pot and increase the heat to medium-high. Stir in the herb bundle along with the pepper, cloves, and nutmeg and cook until they are fragrant, about 30 seconds. Add the wine, then pour in the broth and add the chestnuts. Bring the liquid to a strong simmer, then reduce the heat to medium-low, cover the pot, and simmer, stirring occasionally, until the chestnuts have softened, about 20 minutes. Uncover the pot and remove and discard the herb bundle. Cool the soup for 15 minutes.

4 Add about half of the soup to a blender (or less; you don't want the blender jar more than two-thirds full) along with half of the milk and half of the cream and purée until smooth. Pour the purée into a clean pot and repeat with the remaining soup, milk, and cream.

5 Warm the soup over medium heat and add more broth if you'd like the soup to be thinner. Taste and adjust with additional salt if needed. Ladle the soup into bowls and serve each with a dollop of crème fraîche and a sprinkle of chopped parsley.

MATZAH BALL SOUP

Serves 4 (makes 16 matzah balls)

1 cup plus
2 tablespoons matzah meal (not matzah ball mix)

½ teaspoon baking powder

4 large eggs

¾ teaspoon kosher salt

½ teaspoon freshly ground black pepper, plus extra for serving

2 tablespoons chicken schmaltz (or canola oil in a pinch)

4 quarts store-bought or homemade chicken broth (page 208)

2 tablespoons finely chopped fresh flat-leaf parsley

2 tablespoons finely chopped fresh dill, plus extra for serving

¼ cup plain seltzer water

Thinly sliced carrots and celery, for serving (optional)

According to my mom's side of the family, the perfect matzah ball is fluffy and light—if you're a lover of sinkers, then save your time and look at another recipe. A trio of bubbly seltzer, whipped egg whites, and baking powder keeps the dumplings ethereal and buoyant, while their deep flavor comes from schmaltz (chicken fat) and using chicken broth instead of water in the initial boil, which infuses them with richness. This recipe yields three matzah balls per serving with a few left over for seconds, and let's be realistic, everyone *always* wants seconds.

1 Mix the matzah meal and baking powder in a medium bowl and set aside. Crack the eggs, separating the whites into a large bowl or into the bowl of a stand mixer fitted with the whip attachment and the yolks into a medium bowl. Beat the egg whites until they hold stiff peaks (on medium-high speed if using the mixer). Set aside.

2 Whisk the yolks with the salt and pepper. Add the schmaltz and 2 tablespoons of the chicken broth and whisk to combine. Whisk in the parsley and dill. Add the seltzer, give the mixture a stir (don't stir too much or you'll lose all the fizz!), then add the matzah meal mixture, using a wooden spoon to combine.

3 Whisk in one-quarter of the egg whites to lighten the matzah mixture, then use a rubber spatula or whisk to gently fold in the remaining egg whites until no streaks remain. Place a piece of plastic wrap flush against the mixture and refrigerate for 30 minutes.

4 Using a gentle hand, begin rolling a bit of the mixture between your palms into a matzah ball the size of a golf ball. Try to handle the matzah balls as little as possible to keep

them light. Place the ball on a plate and repeat with the remaining mixture—you should get about 16 matzah balls. Refrigerate the matzah balls for 20 minutes.

5 Pour 8 cups of the chicken broth into a large saucepan or medium pot. Bring the broth to a simmer over medium-high heat. Carefully drop the matzah balls, one at a time, into the gently simmering broth. Cover the pot and gently cook (reduce the heat to low if the broth is simmering too frantically—you don't want your matzah balls to fall apart) until the matzah balls are fluffy and grand, about 45 minutes, stirring them gently about midway through to rotate the balls at the bottom to the top. Turn off the heat.

6 Warm the remaining broth in a medium saucepan with some carrots and celery if you like. Add three matzah balls to each bowl with a ladle or two of broth. Finish with some fresh dill and a twist or two of fresh black pepper and serve.

Joan Nathan's Matzah Balls

A few years back I spent the Fourth of July weekend with friends in Washington, DC. I was introduced to Joan Nathan, the author of many wonderful cookbooks about Jewish cuisine. If anyone knows matzah balls, it's Joan. Joan was one of the people who convinced me that I had to write a cookbook. Her blessing and support were a huge inspiration and gave me the confidence to start thinking seriously about putting my recipes together in a cookbook. And how could I think about matzah balls without thinking about Joan's? Joan has a wonderfully creative streak and loves to breathe new life into traditional and classic recipes. Matzah balls are no exception—Joan is known for adding fresh ginger, dill, *and* nutmeg *to hers!*

STORE-BOUGHT "HOMEMADE" CHICKEN BROTH *Makes about 4 quarts (16 cups) of broth*

4 quarts store-bought chicken broth

4 medium ribs celery, thinly sliced on a bias

2 large carrots, peeled, halved lengthwise, and thinly sliced on a bias

1 large yellow onion, finely chopped

½ cup fresh flat-leaf parsley, finely chopped

In order to build the best flavor foundation, I like to start with a flavorful homemade stock—and if I don't have any in the house, I'll pimp out some store-bought chicken broth to make it taste more homemade. It simulates homemade stock in a fraction of the time—do you have 30 minutes to elevate your cooking? I hope so.

1   Bring the chicken broth to a strong simmer in a large pot over medium-high heat.

2   Add the celery, carrots, onion, and parsley, reduce the heat to medium-low, and gently simmer until the vegetables are very tender, about 30 minutes.

3   Taste the broth and add salt or pepper if needed. Strain out the vegetables and discard (unless you like very soft vegetables!). Cool the broth to room temperature, then transfer to an airtight container and refrigerate for up to 1 week, or transfer to resealable freezer bags to freeze for up to 6 months.

ACCESSORIZE YOUR BROTH

A simple addition of herbs or spice can give your broth just the twist you need, giving it the change of flavor direction from, say, the broth you use to accent risotto (page 34) to the broth you use to make matzah ball soup (page 206) or the broth for a Caribbean lobster curry (page 107). Here are some ideas to get you thinking.

In step 2, with the parsley, add your choice of:

Bay leaf

Cinnamon stick

Cloves

Coriander seeds

Dried red chile peppers

Ginger slices

Juniper berries

Lemongrass

Makrut lime leaf

Thyme sprigs

In step 2, for the last 5 minutes of cooking, add your choice of:

Basil sprigs

Chervil

Dill sprigs

Fennel fronds

Rosemary sprigs

Sage leaves

Slices of fresh green chile peppers

Strip of lemon, lime, or orange zest

Tarragon sprigs

Turmeric

KABOCHA SQUASH SOUP WITH CROUTONS

Serves 4 to 6

Soup
2 tablespoons extra-virgin olive oil

1 large yellow onion, chopped

1 teaspoon sea salt

½ medium celery root, peeled and chopped

1 medium carrot, peeled and chopped

4 pounds winter squash, preferably kabocha, peeled, seeded, and chopped into 1" chunks

¼ cup red miso paste

Croutons
3 cups bite-size bread cubes (preferably cut from a day-old baguette)

1½ tablespoons extra-virgin olive oil

½ teaspoon sea salt

Whagh I'm traveling to present collections around the world or on set shooting episodes of *Project Runway*, I'm often eating foods from catering services. While these meals are good, they're often not the cleanest foods to eat—meaning they're heavily dressed or salted and not as nutrient-rich as the foods I like to eat. So when I'm at home, I crave simple, clean foods, and this puréed squash soup is one of the healthiest, purest recipes in this book. It counts on kabocha squash, a hard winter squash, for its rich sweetness and creamy texture—it's truly my favorite winter vegetable. Miso paste adds soulful umami, while onion, carrot, and celery root counter the sweetness of the squash with their savory qualities.

1 *To make the soup:* Heat the olive oil in a large soup pot over medium heat. Add the onion and ½ teaspoon of the salt and cook, stirring often, until the onion is soft but not browned, about 5 minutes. Stir in the celery root and carrot, then add 4 cups of water, the squash, and the remaining ½ teaspoon of salt.

2 Increase the heat to high and bring the water to a simmer. Cover the pot and cook until the squash is tender, about 15 minutes. Turn off the heat and leave the pot covered for 15 minutes.

3 *To make the croutons:* Meanwhile, preheat the oven to 400°F. Toss the bread cubes with the olive oil and salt in a large bowl. Turn them out onto a rimmed sheet pan and toast in the oven until they are golden brown, 5 to 8 minutes. Remove from the oven and transfer to a large plate.

4 Pour some of the soup into a blender (don't fill the blender more than two-thirds full so the pressure buildup from the heat of the soup doesn't cause the top to blow off!). Blend the soup with half of the miso, then pour into a clean pot. Blend the remaining soup with the remaining miso and add to the pot. Warm over medium-low heat until the soup is hot, then divide into bowls and serve with plenty of croutons on top.

UNI PASTA *Serves 4*

1 pound spaghetti

1 tablespoon plus
¼ teaspoon fine sea salt

¼ pound (about ¾ cup)
shelled uni (sea urchin)

¼ cup extra-virgin
olive oil

2 tablespoons heavy
cream

½ teaspoon freshly
ground black pepper

⅛ teaspoon cayenne
pepper

2 tablespoons unsalted
butter

2 tablespoons finely
chopped fresh chives

Buying Uni

*Sea urchin, also called
uni in Japanese, must be
eaten within hours of
shucking from its spiky
shell. In France, you can
buy fresh sea urchin at
the daily outdoor mar-
kets. Here in New York
City, that's not an option,
so I buy mine from the
Japanese market close to
my apartment in Man-
hattan. Sushi restaurants
also often sell uni, so you
can always buy a few
pieces.*

Pulled from the sea floor, spiky sea urchin looks impenetra-
ble upon first glance, but break open the spiny shell and
you are confronted with this apricot-colored creature that
tastes like a pure combination of sea air and soft ocean brine.
Here I turn it into a quick sauce by adding the shelled uni to a
food processor and puréeing it with some olive oil, cream, and
pepper. I first ate pasta this way, which is kind of like a car-
bonara of the sea (in which uni replaces the porky guanciale or
pancetta), at a little restaurant on the Sardinian coast where
fishermen plucked pristine uni from the cobalt sea. The lovely
thing is that it's also very quick and easy to make, the only
catch being that the pasta must be served immediately after
tossing with the uni sauce—as the dish sits, the delicate sauce
can lose its silkiness, so definitely dig right in after plating!

1 Bring a large pot of water to a boil. Add the spaghetti and
1 tablespoon of the salt and cook according to package direc-
tions until the spaghetti is al dente. Reserve ¾ cup of pasta
water, then drain the pasta and set it aside.

2 Add the uni, olive oil, cream, black pepper, the remaining
¼ teaspoon of salt, and the cayenne to the bowl of a food processor and process until completely smooth.

3 Add the butter to the pasta pot and set it over medium heat.
Once the butter is melted, add the pasta water and turn off the
heat. Return the pasta to the pot and toss with the butter-water
mixture. Quickly add the uni purée and 1½ tablespoons of the
chives, give it a very quick stir, and be speedy about turning the
pasta out into a large serving bowl (work quickly because if
overcooked, the uni will curdle like scrambled eggs). Sprinkle
the remaining ½ tablespoon of chives over the top of the pasta
and serve immediately.

KUNG PAO SHRIMP *Serves 4*

¼ cup granulated sugar

¼ cup distilled white vinegar

¼ cup soy sauce

1 pound 16/20 shrimp, peeled, deveined, and dried with paper towels

¼ cup cornstarch

1 cup peanut oil

12 garlic cloves, very finely minced

1 piece (2" long) fresh gingerroot, peeled and finely chopped

8 scallions, green parts only, sliced on a bias into 1" pieces

Steamed white rice, for serving

This dish is one of my mom's signature dishes; she makes it frequently throughout the year, but always, *always* at New Year's. My dad likes things that are sweet and sour, so Kung Pao Shrimp fits the bill. It must be eaten just after it is cooked in the wok. It's good served with white rice or clear noodles— something that will take up the delicious sauce.

1 Whisk together the sugar, vinegar, and soy sauce in a medium bowl until the sugar is dissolved. Set aside.

2 Line a large plate with a paper towel and set aside. Add the dried shrimp to a medium bowl and toss with the cornstarch. Heat the peanut oil in a wok or slope-sided large and deep skillet over high heat until it just starts to smoke, about 2 minutes. Add a shrimp—it should be immediately surrounded by bubbles (if it isn't, continue to heat the oil until bubbles engulf the shrimp). Continue adding the shrimp to the pan quickly but one at a time. Cook, turning them often with tongs, until they are tightly curled, 1 to 2 minutes. Use a slotted spoon or frying spider to transfer the shrimp to the paper towel–lined plate.

3 Add the garlic and ginger to the pan and cook, stirring often, until it is very fragrant and just starting to take on color, about 2 minutes. Pour in the soy-vinegar mixture and bring it to a simmer. Return the shrimp to the pan and toss to coat until the sauce is thick and glossy, about 2 minutes. Turn off the heat and transfer the shrimp to a platter. Serve sprinkled with scallions and with rice on the side.

A QUICK TRIP TO CHINA

SoHo in lower Manhattan is all about glitzy shops, trendy boutiques, and fine restaurants these days. But growing up in SoHo in the 1980s was different—you felt as if you lived on the fringe of the city because *no one* came south of Houston (unless you worked all the way south in the Financial District on Wall Street). Those of us who lived there back then, primarily artists and their families, most of whom knew one another, would attend openings at neighborhood galleries with people spilling out onto the street. I can tell you that growing up in SoHo was nothing short of magical—it felt like a creative Wild Wild West: artists and lofts, playgrounds and rooftops, pizza parlors and a couple of unfashionable yet delicious bistros where you could get escargot and beef tartare.

Some of my favorite memories are of going with my dad to Chinatown, which was only a few blocks south of our loft on Spring Street. It was like a giant open-air market for buying a slew of Chinese provisions and goods. My dad and I used to walk over to pick up ingredients for dinner like dried shrimp the size of your pinky fingertip and unidentifiable dried or fermented things in large bins right on the street. There were vendors selling fresh tofu from earthenware pots, fresh fish, bins of leafy greens, mangoes of many shapes and sizes, spiky kidney-shaped durian, brown clusters of longan fruit that looked like parchment paper–covered grapes, bright magenta dragon fruit, and, when in season, lychee fruit. Even today, as SoHo has changed from an artistic enclave to a high-end shopping center, it comforts me that the Chinatown of my youth is still intact (aside from the tour buses that roll through). I'll often walk around for ideas for a dinner party or to stoke my imagination to get me thinking about a new ingredient or dish. I love that inspiration exists around every corner in New York and that there are always new markets and new ingredients to discover and fall in love with.

CITRUS AND SPICE THANKSGIVING DUCK

Serves 6

Steaming Tisane

6 tangerines or clementines, quartered

2 large pieces (each about 5" long) fresh gingerroot, sliced into thin rounds

8 allspice berries

8 cardamom pods

4 star anise pods

2 cinnamon sticks

Duck

1 Pekin (Long Island) duck (5½ pounds), excess fat removed from the cavity and neck removed

1 head garlic, cloves separated and peeled

3 star anise pods

Peel from 2 lemons, any white pith on the peel removed, 1 lemon halved (save the other lemon for the glaze)

1 piece (1" long) fresh gingerroot, peeled and roughly chopped

1 tablespoon fresh thyme leaves

1 tablespoon kosher salt

1 teaspoon freshly ground black pepper

10 kumquats, halved

12 whole cloves

ingredients continue

There is something so expected about making a turkey for Thanksgiving . . . which is why I choose to cook both a turkey *and* a duck! Duck is tender and flavorful, and just generally more succulent than a turkey. It is a smaller fowl, but you can always roast two to supplement if you decide to forgo the turkey. The key to keeping the meat moist is to give the duck an initial steam using a spiced tisane. After steaming, I poke holes in the skin all over the surface of the duck and then score the skin and fat in a cross-hatch pattern (without cutting into the meat) to allow the fat to render off while simultaneously making the skin crackling-crisp. The glaze is based on a sweet Indonesian sauce called ketjap manis. It's aromatic, thick, and dark, kind of like an Indonesian ketchup. You can find it in the international aisle of most supermarkets, in Asian markets, and online.

---

1 *To make the steaming tisane:* Fill a large pot with 4 quarts (16 cups) of water. Add the tangerines, ginger, allspice, cardamom, star anise, and cinnamon sticks and bring to a boil. Reduce the heat to a gentle simmer and cook for 30 minutes to infuse the water. Turn off the heat.

2 *To make the duck:* Preheat the oven to 300°F. Rinse the duck under cold water and pat the outside and inside dry. Add the garlic, star anise, lemon peel, ginger, thyme, salt, and pepper to the small bowl insert of a food processor. Process until the garlic is very finely puréed, then massage the rub into the cavity and over the skin of the duck. Squeeze the kumquats into the cavity of the duck and add them to the cavity, then repeat with one lemon half, squeezing the juice in and then adding the squeezed fruit to the cavity. Stick the sharp end of the cloves into the breast and legs, tuck the wings behind the backbone

recipe continues

Hoisin Glaze

½ cup hoisin sauce

¼ cup ketjap manis

¼ cup orange juice
(preferably freshly
squeezed)

Juice of 1 lemon

2 tablespoons honey

½ teaspoon freshly
ground black pepper

(just as you would to roast a chicken), and use twine or a piece of aluminum foil folded into a "rope" to tie the base of the legs together.

3 Set a roasting rack into a roasting pan (preferably a flat rack). Add enough of the steaming tisane to cover the pan, but don't let the liquid touch the bottom of the roasting rack. Place the duck on the rack breast side down, cover the roasting pan with a few sheets of foil, and roast the duck in the oven for 1 hour.

4 *To make the glaze:* While the duck roasts, whisk together the hoisin sauce, ketjap manis, orange juice, lemon juice, honey, and pepper in a small bowl. Set aside.

5 Remove the roasting pan from the oven and carefully peel the foil away from you (take care as you don't want the hot steam to billow up into your face). Fold up two bunches of paper towels and use them to flip the duck breast side up. Use a sharp knife to prick about a dozen holes just through the skin and fat (don't slice into the meat) all over the duck (especially in the joint where the leg connects to the body), then use the knife to score the breast, making slits through the skin and fat just down to the meat (don't slice through the meat) about ½" apart. Angle the knife in the opposite direction and repeat to get a cross-hatch pattern over each breast. Increase the oven temperature to 450°F.

6 Use a basting brush to coat the entire duck with the glaze. Return the roasting pan to the oven and roast the duck, glazing every 15 minutes, until the temperature in the thigh reaches 160°F, about 35 to 45 minutes longer.

7 Remove the duck from the oven and set aside for 10 minutes, then carefully tip it (so the wide cavity opening faces the roasting pan) over the roasting pan to drain off any juices from the cavity. Place the duck on a cutting board, breast side up, and carve. Pour the pan juices into a fat separator and remove as much fat as possible, then serve the pan sauce on the side.

CRANBERRY–ORANGE RELISH *Makes about 2 cups*

1 navel orange, well washed (unpeeled)

4 cups fresh cranberries

1 cup granulated sugar

Finely grated zest of ½ lemon

We always have at least four varieties of cranberry sauce on our Thanksgiving table: the one from the can (which I happen to love, so don't knock it!), a cooked saucy version or whatever Uncle Dan is making, some sort of chutney experiment from my mom, and a raw relish like this one. It's so fresh and bright and citrusy that it just wakes up the palate between bites of the delicious and rich foods on your plate. If I have any left over, I'll add it to muffin or quick bread batter.

1 Cut the orange in half, then cut each half into quarters, rind and all. Place the orange pieces in a blender jar or the bowl of a food processor fitted with the metal blade.

2 Add the cranberries, sugar, and lemon zest and process until the mixture is semi-smooth. Be careful—you still want texture.

3 Transfer to an airtight container and refrigerate until serving. The relish stays delicious for up to 5 days.

THANKSGIVING
WITH THE POSENS

Our table is always set for family, friends, and anyone who happens to be in town—no one should be without a Thanksgiving meal! Mom insists on recipes that pay honor to tradition and have a family provenance. So, despite getting a lot of derision, she continues to this day to make a green lime Jell-O mold using a recipe from her mother-in-law, my Grandma Shubie. I'm guessing it probably came from a 1950s *Ladies' Home Journal*! The lime Jell-O is combined with cucumber and crushed pineapple. Then there's the cranberry sauce that my Uncle Dan makes. His recipe comes from his Southern family and is very citrusy. As for the turkey, we have tried cooking it every which way: fresh, frozen, deep-fried, brined, and smoked. It is always good, but me being me, I've begun presenting a Thanksgiving duck on the table as well, because why not? If you can't indulge in excess on Thanksgiving, when can you? Family opinions vary wildly on the issue of stuffing: Should the stuffing be "in the body" or come from an "out-of-body" experience? The current preference is to use a muffin pan to achieve the maximum amount of crispy top crust because of the increased surface area.

In the morning, before I get too deep into cooking, I make decorating our dining room a priority. I close the double doors to the dining room and let no one come in. Sometimes I'll bring flowers from a florist, but mostly I take clippers and go outside and bring in leaves and branches, pinecones, and anything that I can forage. I might add some tiny lights or candles. One of my favorite tactics is to hang things from the chandelier, like pine or fir branches, or sprigs of autumn berries. I can honestly say that I strive for excess! The thrill of throwing open the dining room doors when it's time to sit down to the feast is unparalleled. We traditionally start the meal with everyone singing "Simple Gifts," a beautiful Shaker hymn that reminds everyone of the gifts we enjoy. I love the line " 'Tis the gift to come down where we ought to be." I think it sets a graceful tone for the entire holiday season.

PROSCIUTTO-WRAPPED CHATEAUBRIAND *Serves 4 to 6*

1 center-cut trimmed and tied beef tenderloin (2 pounds)

3 medium garlic cloves, finely chopped

2 heaping tablespoons roughly chopped fresh flat-leaf parsley

2 heaping tablespoons roughly chopped fresh rosemary

1 sprig fresh thyme, plus 1 heaping teaspoon finely chopped fresh thyme

1 tablespoon coarse sea salt

1 teaspoon freshly ground black pepper

2 tablespoons extra-virgin olive oil

8 ounces thinly sliced prosciutto

½ cup beef broth

1 tablespoon unsalted butter

Filet mignon is cut from the beef tenderloin, a tender length of meat that is the most prime and pricey cut of beef. The French name for the whole roast is a Chateaubriand, named after Monsieur François René de Chateaubriand, the father of French literary Romanticism—sounds so fancy and elegant! I like to wrap the whole roast in thin leaves of prosciutto before roasting to really send the presentation over the top, making this a fantastic choice for a swank New Year's Eve dinner party or even a fancy Christmas dinner. I've also used high-quality thinly sliced smoked bacon instead of prosciutto with great results. If there are any leftovers, thin slices of the Chateaubriand are wonderful with horseradish mayonnaise served on a dark bread, which also happens to make a fine hors d'oeuvre.

1 Remove the beef roast from the refrigerator and place it on a cutting board or plate. Let the tenderloin rest at room temperature for 30 minutes before preheating the oven to 425°F. Add the garlic, parsley, rosemary, chopped thyme, salt, pepper, and olive oil to the small bowl insert of a food processor and pulse into a rough paste. Place the tenderloin on a cutting board and pat it dry with a paper towel, then rub the paste all over the tenderloin. Scooch the tenderloin to one side of the board.

2 Place a large sheet of plastic wrap on the cutting board. Starting at one end of the plastic wrap, overlap six prosciutto slices so the short end faces you (so the piece of prosciutto lies vertically on the wrap). Make sure you don't overlap them too much—you want the finished sheet of overlapping prosciutto pieces to be about the same length as your roast. With the remaining two slices of prosciutto, wrap each end of the roast, then set the roast on top of the prosciutto layer and roll it to wrap it snugly. It should be completely enclosed. Fasten the roast with a few pieces of butcher's twine at 1" intervals so it keeps a nice round shape as it roasts.

3 Set the wrapped tenderloin in a roasting pan and roast until the prosciutto is browned and crisp and an instant-read ther-

mometer inserted into the center reads 122° to 125°F for rare (125° to 128°F for medium-rare), 25 to 30 minutes. Remove the roasting pan from the oven and transfer the roast to a cutting board (you'll use the pan drippings in the next step, so don't wash the pan!). Loosely tent the roast with aluminum foil to keep it warm while it rests for 15 minutes.

4 Pour the pan drippings from the roasting pan into a medium saucepan. Add the beef broth and the thyme sprig and bring the juices to a simmer over medium-high heat. Reduce the heat to medium-low and whisk in the butter. Once the butter is melted, turn off the heat and remove and discard the thyme sprig.

5 To serve, snip off the twine, then slice the tenderloin crosswise into ½"-thick pieces and fan them out on a platter. Serve the "au jus" on the side in a gravy boat.

Keys to a Perfect Roast (or Steak!)

When I eat meat, I want it to be spot-on. High-quality humanely raised and preferably organic beef is a high-ticket item, especially if you're serving it for a dinner party where you can't get away with one steak sliced out to serve two or three people, but need to present something celebratory and grand. Here are some tips I've learned that really make a difference!

- For even, faster cooking and a more beautiful crust-to-interior color gradation (no gray meat!), let the meat sit out, uncovered, on a pan at room temperature for 30 minutes to 1 hour before cooking.

- Pat the roast dry before cooking to encourage as much browning of the crust as possible (this is especially important if you're doing any pan searing).

- Let the roast rest for 15 minutes before slicing to allow the juices to be reabsorbed into the meat (otherwise, they will spill out onto your cutting board).

- Always slice meat against the grain for the most tender bite.

CREAMED SPINACH *Serves 4*

2 tablespoons unsalted butter

2 garlic cloves, thinly sliced

2 tablespoons all-purpose flour

1 cup heavy cream

¼ cup store-bought or homemade chicken broth (page 208), vegetable broth, or water

¼ teaspoon freshly grated nutmeg

½ teaspoon fine sea salt

¼ teaspoon freshly ground black pepper

8 cups large-leaf spinach, stems removed and leaves roughly chopped

¼ cup finely grated Parmigiano-Reggiano cheese

Wash Those Greens

Leafy greens often have lots of dirt lodged in between leaves or around the stem end. I like to cover them with cold water and swish them around. Then I lift them out, place them in a colander, rinse the bowl with water, and repeat twice. Do not pour the greens and the water into a colander—it's key to lift the greens out first— otherwise, you're pouring the dirty water right back over your washed greens.

This recipe is my take on the creamed spinach from the infamously scruffy and gruff yet unparalleled Brooklyn steakhouse Peter Luger's. During my first week of high school at St. Ann's in Brooklyn, some friends took me there, and I have to say, the experience was life changing. The porterhouse steak was sublime! It came out of the kitchen sizzling hot, and the servers sliced it off the T-bone tableside and then seared it a little extra on the side of the platter (it's that hot!). Besides steak, Luger's is known for its sides, like creamed spinach, the bacon (yes, a slab of bacon is considered an appetizer), and their steak sauce (sold in grocery stores and corner bodegas throughout the city). The secret to the spinach is lots of cream, of course, and resisting the temptation to cook the spinach to death. Fresh spinach is a must to retain that bright green color. The creamed spinach is so good that I love it without the steak and just with great bread on the side.

1 Melt the butter in a large skillet over medium-high heat. Let the butter cook until it smells nutty and turns light brown, 2 to 3 minutes.

2 Stir in the garlic and cook until it is fragrant, about 30 seconds, then reduce the heat to medium-low and stir in the flour, making sure to work out any lumps. Cook the flour until it turns a medium golden brown color, about 2 minutes.

3 Whisk in half of the cream (it will quickly become like a paste), then whisk in the remaining cream and chicken broth. Stir in the nutmeg, salt, and pepper and then add the spinach, using a spoon to stir it into the sauce until the spinach wilts, 2 to 3 minutes. Stir in the cheese and turn off the heat. Taste and season with more salt if needed. Transfer to a serving dish and serve immediately.

CRISPY THREE–POTATO LATKES *Makes about 16 small latkes*

2 large russet potatoes (about 1½ pounds)

1 medium purple potato (or an extra russet; about 10 ounces)

1 small sweet potato (about 6 ounces)

1 large yellow onion, peeled

½ cup all-purpose flour or matzah meal

1 teaspoon baking powder

1 tablespoon coarse sea salt, plus extra as needed

¼ teaspoon freshly ground black pepper

1½ cups vegetable or peanut oil

2 large eggs, well beaten

2 tablespoons finely chopped fresh chives

¼ cup crème fraîche or sour cream

1 jar (3 ounces) salmon roe or a couple of slices of smoked salmon, cut into bits (optional)

Finely chopped fresh dill, for serving

Just about every person who celebrates Hanukkah has a technique for making the best latkes. My contribution to the fray is to add color (what a surprise from a fashion designer!). Though latkes are traditionally served around the winter holidays, there's no reason not to serve them in the spring or summer—they're fantastic as the hash brown/home fry component of a brunch, too (keep them warm and crisp on a wire cooling rack set over a sheet pan in a 200°F oven for up to 1 hour). The toppings here, crème fraîche, salmon roe, and dill, are pretty high end. Latkes are also fantastic with Greek yogurt, smoked and flaked salmon, or chutney; sprinkled with za'atar; or served with simple applesauce (page 173).

1 Fit a food processor with the grater attachment (or use the medium-hole side of a box grater; if using a box grater, leave the potatoes whole). Quarter the potatoes lengthwise and, with the food processor running, press them through the grater attachment. Repeat with the onion.

2 Place the grated potatoes and onion in cheesecloth or a clean kitchen towel and squeeze out the liquid into a bowl. Place the solids in a separate medium bowl. Let the liquid squeezed out from the potatoes settle for 10 minutes so the potato starch sinks to the bottom of the bowl. Pour off the water, but keep the potato starch at the bottom.

3 Whisk together the flour, baking powder, salt, and pepper in a small bowl. Set aside. Add the vegetable or peanut oil to a large cast-iron skillet (or a heavy-bottomed skillet) and heat it over high heat until it starts to shimmer.

recipe continues

4 Add the reserved potato starch, eggs, and chives to the grated potato and onion mixture and stir to combine. Stir in the flour mixture.

5 Use your hands to cup and press out a silver dollar–size potato patty and place on a plate. Repeat with the remaining potato mixture. Add a few pancakes to the hot oil and use the back of a spoon to flatten them out. Fry until deeply browned and crisp, about 5 minutes. Then turn with a fork and fry the other side until browned, 3 to 4 minutes longer. Use a spatula to transfer the latke to a paper towel–lined plate or wire rack set over a paper bag to drain while you fry the remaining latkes.

6 Sprinkle with salt and serve dolloped with crème fraîche and salmon roe and finished with a bit of dill.

MASHED SEMI–SWEETS

Serves 6

3 medium sweet potatoes (about 1¾ pounds), unpeeled

1 medium russet potato, unpeeled

1 tablespoon plus 1 teaspoon sea salt, plus extra as needed

3 tablespoons unsalted butter, melted and still warm

1½ cups heavy cream, warmed

My trick to the best mashed sweet potatoes ever is to include one russet potato—it helps to aerate the otherwise somewhat naturally watery texture of sweet potatoes and also curbs the intense sweetness. Cooking the potatoes skin-on keeps the texture fluffy once the potatoes are mashed rather than heavy and waterlogged. I like to peel the potatoes while they are still warm—not only does the skin slip off easily, but, with a pinch of salt, the skins make a great snack. A potato ricer is a key investment not just for mashed potatoes but also for gnocchi (pages 149 and 152). Sometimes I like to infuse the cream with sage or rosemary or even a vanilla bean pod to add an extra dimension of flavor to the mashed sweets.

1 Fill a large pot with cold water. Add the potatoes and 1 tablespoon of the salt and bring the water to a boil over high heat. Reduce the heat to medium and gently boil the potatoes until a paring knife easily slips into the center of the largest one, 20 to 25 minutes. Drain the potatoes and set them aside until they are cool enough to handle (but not too cool), then peel them.

2 Place the potatoes in a potato ricer (or use a food mill) and press them through into a large bowl. Use a whisk to stir in the melted butter and the remaining 1 teaspoon of salt, then whisk in the cream. Taste and add more salt if needed.

GRANDMA JEANNE'S BUTTERSCOTCH WAFERS *Makes 3 dozen cookies*

1½ cups chopped
walnuts

1¼ cups all-purpose
flour

1½ teaspoons baking
powder

½ teaspoon fine sea
salt

½ cup (1 stick)
unsalted butter, at
room temperature

2 cups lightly packed
dark brown sugar

2 large eggs

This is a great holiday cookie because you can make a giant batch of dough and bake the cookies off all at once or keep logs in the freezer and bake them off when company is expected. One of my fondest food memories is making butterscotch-walnut cookies with my mom from a terrific recipe of my Great-Grandmother Jeanne Hirsch, who grew up in South Carolina. Jeanne, I was told, would roll the dough into long logs and wrap them in waxed paper for chilling before baking—something I still do. My mom remembers being at Girl Scout camp and receiving a shoebox tied up with string from her grandmother filled with these delicious cookies. They melt in your mouth and are best when they are very thin, with crisp and browned edges. Be warned—they are addictive!

1 Preheat the oven to 350°F. Place the walnuts on a rimmed sheet pan and toast them in the oven until fragrant, 8 to 10 minutes. Transfer the walnuts to a plate and set them aside.

2 Whisk the flour, baking powder, and salt together in a medium bowl. Add the butter and brown sugar to the bowl of a stand mixer and cream together on medium-low speed until combined. Increase the mixer speed to medium-high and beat the mixture until light and creamy, about 2 minutes. Reduce the mixer speed to medium-low and add the eggs, one at a time, mixing well after each addition and using a rubber spatula to scrape the bottom and sides of the bowl as needed.

3 Stop the mixer, add the flour mixture, and mix on low speed until the flour is nearly incorporated. Add the walnuts and continue to mix until there aren't any streaks of flour in the cookie dough.

4 Place about half of the dough in the center of a piece of parchment or waxed paper and use the paper to help you shape the dough into a 2"-wide log. Roll the log back and forth so the

sides are nicely rounded. Repeat with the remaining dough to make two logs. Set the parchment-wrapped logs on a baking sheet and freeze them until hard, about 2 hours.

5 Preheat the oven to 375°F. Unwrap a log and place it on a cutting board. Use a sharp knife to slice the log crosswise into the thinnest possible rounds without having the cookie crumble apart—about ⅛" to 1/16" thick. Set the cookies 1½" apart on a parchment paper–lined baking sheet and bake until golden around the edges, 10 to 12 minutes. Remove from the oven and cool for 5 minutes before using a spatula to transfer the cookies to a wire rack. Bake as many cookies as you need and wrap the leftover logs in plastic wrap, then place them in a resealable freezer bag to bake off another time.

Fresh Baked on Demand

Who says you have to bake two dozen cookies at once? It can be a nice treat to freeze some and bake them off when you get a craving, or when that perfect moment comes up and a fresh-baked cookie is called for. Simply freeze the logs or dough balls on a plate until semihard, about 20 minutes, then transfer them to a resealable freezer bag and freeze for up to 6 months. To bake, just follow the instructions in step 5, above—they may need an extra minute or two in the oven.

DARK STOUT CRÊPES

Makes 12 crêpes

1 cup all-purpose flour

2 tablespoons cornstarch

2 tablespoons granulated sugar

¼ teaspoon fine sea salt

2 large eggs

2 tablespoons canola or grapeseed oil

2 teaspoons vanilla extract

1½ cups milk, warmed to room temperature

1 cup dark stout beer

6 tablespoons unsalted butter, melted

I like to have some crêpe batter stashed in the refrigerator over long holiday stretches when hosting friends and family overnight. Crêpes make a quick and simple breakfast, brunch, lunch, dinner, or even dessert that never fails to make someone feel special. The batter holds in the refrigerator really well, too, and the crêpes are even more beautiful and delicious if the batter rests overnight before you make them (this allows you to get a thinner crêpe that won't crack—the batter can be refrigerated for up to 3 days). You can serve them folded around ham and cheese, creamed spinach (page 224), or sautéed mushrooms, or with jam or store-bought Meyer lemon curd. Sometimes I will just sprinkle them with white sugar before folding into quarters and serving. You can even use the crêpes to make a mille-crêpe cake with chestnut cream filling (see box on next page).

1 Whisk the flour, cornstarch, sugar, and salt together in a large bowl. Whisk together the eggs, canola or grapeseed oil, and vanilla in a medium bowl.

2 Whisk the egg mixture into the flour mixture until thick and smooth. Whisk the milk in a little at a time to thin the paste, then whisk in the beer and 4 tablespoons of the melted butter until the batter is smooth. Cover the top with plastic wrap and let it sit out at room temperature for 2 hours (or refrigerate overnight, then let it sit out at room temperature for 1 hour before using).

3 Heat an 8" or 9" skillet over medium-high heat. Add 1 teaspoon of the remaining melted butter to the pan, then add about ¼ cup of batter, tilting the pan to swirl the batter around until it makes a thin and even circular crêpe. Cook until the underside of the crêpe is golden brown, 1½ to 2 minutes (reduce the heat if it is browning too quickly), then use a metal spatula or a quick jerking motion to flip the crêpe over to the other side. Cook on the other side until just golden brown

in spots, 30 seconds to 1 minute. Slide the crêpe onto a plate. Repeat with the remaining batter, using the remaining butter as needed. (You can create a stack of crêpes without worrying about them sticking together.)

4 Serve with your filling of choice. You can serve the crêpes flat and round, roll them into a cylinder, or fold them in half and then half again to make a folded triangle shape.

Chestnut Cream Crêpe Cake

Double the recipe for Dark Stout Crêpes and use a 9" skillet to cook the crêpes. Make a double batch of the chestnut cream on page 247. Line the bottom of a springform pan with a circle of parchment paper and place a crêpe flat on top. Spread ¼ cup of chestnut cream over the crêpe, using an offset spatula to spread the cream as evenly as possible. Set another crêpe on top. Repeat until all of the chestnut cream and crêpes are used. Cover the top of the cake pan with plastic wrap and refrigerate the cake for at least 2 hours before unclasping the springform mold, dusting the top with powdered sugar (or cocoa powder), slicing, and serving.

PFEFFERNÜESSE COOKIES *Makes about 2 dozen cookies*

2 cups packed dark brown sugar

2 large eggs

½ teaspoon baking soda

2½ cups bread flour, sifted

1 teaspoon ground cardamom

¼ teaspoon ground cloves

¼ teaspoon ground mace

¼ teaspoon fine sea salt

1 cup chopped nuts (pecans, walnuts, almonds, and hazelnuts are all good options)

2 cups powdered sugar, for finishing the cookies

The atelier is positively electric once the winter holidays are upon us, with everyone eagerly anticipating the office holiday party. I always bring Christmas cookies—usually gingerbread (page 255) and other holiday treats like these pfeffernüesse cookies with mace, rather than pepper. Pfeffernüesse are great because I can make them in minutes. All they need is an hour in the fridge to chill before shaping and baking. It's a simple and delicious way to care for the people who care for me all year long.

1 Whisk the brown sugar and eggs together in a large bowl until foamy. Stir together the baking soda and 1 tablespoon of hot water in a small bowl, then whisk it into the beaten egg mixture.

2 Place a fine-mesh sieve over the egg mixture. Add the flour, cardamom, cloves, mace, and salt to the sieve and sift into the egg mixture. Use a wooden spoon to stir in the nuts. Cover the bowl with plastic wrap and refrigerate until it is stiff enough to easily handle and shape into balls, about 1 hour.

3 Preheat the oven to 325°F. Scoop about 1 tablespoon of dough from the bowl, roll it into a ball, and set it on a parchment paper–lined rimmed baking sheet. Repeat, leaving 1" between balls. Bake the cookies off in two batches of 12 cookies per baking sheet. Bake until firm to the touch, 8 to 10 minutes.

4 Remove from the oven and cool for 2 minutes. Place the powdered sugar in a medium bowl and add a few cookies to it, rolling them through the sugar to coat them on all sides (it's important to do this while the cookies are still warm). Place the sugared cookies on a wire rack to cool completely. Repeat with the remaining dough. Store the cookies in neat layers separated by waxed paper or parchment and in an airtight container to preserve their flavor and texture. They'll last for a week, if not longer!

CHOCOLATE GANACHE AND ALMOND MERINGUE CAKE

Makes a 3-layer meringue cake serving 10 to 12

Meringue Layers
6 ounces (about 1½ cups) blanched, slivered almonds

10 large egg whites

1 teaspoon vanilla or almond extract

1¾ cups granulated sugar

1 tablespoon cornstarch

Ganache
8 ounces good-quality semisweet chocolate chips (about 1¼ cups)

⅔ cup heavy cream

Whipped Cream and Assembly
2¼ cups heavy cream

½ cup granulated sugar

1 teaspoon vanilla extract

3 tablespoons powdered sugar

½ cup fruit preserves (such as apricot, berry, or cherry)

Note: You will need two half sheet pans to bake the meringues.

Who doesn't love cake? Especially when the cake layers are made from sweet and crunchy gluten-free meringue layers rather than traditional cake layers made with flour! This dessert is a pure showstopper—as beautiful as she is delicious. It is a bit of a production to make, but you can prepare it in stages, just like a finale gown in a runway show. The sweet meringue layers are sandwiched with fudgy chocolate ganache and a surprise layer of preserves (my favorite in this cake is apricot, but cherry or berry is also delicious). Anyone with a sweet tooth will melt over this pièce de résistance.

1 *To start the meringue layers:* Adjust one oven rack to the upper-middle position and another to the lower-middle position. Preheat the oven to 350°F. Place the almonds on a rimmed sheet pan and toast on the lower-middle rack until lightly browned, 7 to 8 minutes, shaking the pan midway through toasting (keep an eye on the almonds as they can go from perfect to too dark in a flash). Transfer the almonds to a plate and set aside to cool. Once cool, add the almonds to the bowl of a food processor and pulse until they are roughly chopped (you don't want them too fine like a meal or flour). Reduce the oven temperature to 250°F.

2 Trim two pieces of parchment paper to fit two half sheet pans (you'll bake off two meringue circles on one pan and one on the other pan with the decorative meringue buttons). Place an 8" or 9" plate or cake pan on the parchment paper and use a pencil to trace a circle around it. Remove and repeat—this will be your template for the meringue layers. Repeat on the other piece of parchment one time for the third layer. Turn the paper over so the pencil doesn't mark the layers and set the sheet pans aside.

recipe continues

3 Add the egg whites and vanilla to the bowl of a stand mixer fitted with the whisk attachment (or a large bowl if using a hand mixer) and beat on medium-high speed until they begin to get frothy. Gradually sprinkle in ¾ cup of the granulated sugar and continue to beat until the whites hold stiff peaks (about 2 minutes). You can test the whites by stopping the mixer and dipping the whisk into the frothy whites, then pulling it out. The whites should form stiff and pointy peaks that don't droop.

4 Mix the remaining 1 cup of granulated sugar and the cornstarch together in a medium bowl, then whisk in the ground almonds. Use a rubber spatula to fold the almond mixture into the meringue until the mixture is well blended. Place a round pastry tip into a pastry bag (or snip a 1" opening from the corner of a gallon-size resealable plastic bag) and add some of the meringue mixture. Starting at the center of the circle, pipe the meringue in a circular motion spiraling toward the outer edge. Repeat with the other two circles and then pipe six 1" meringue buttons that will be used for decoration. (You can also use the rounded bottom part of a spoon to dollop meringue onto the paper and smooth out the top in a circular motion, taking care not to flatten the meringue too much.)

5 Bake the meringues until they are barely golden and dry, about 45 minutes for the small buttons (remove them using a spatula and transfer to a wire rack to cool) and 1½ hours for the larger disks, switching the sheet pans from top to bottom and vice versa midway through baking (after you remove the small buttons is a good time to make the switch). Remove the sheet pans from the oven and set aside to cool completely before removing the meringues from the sheet pan (leave them on the parchment paper). (At this point, the meringue layers can be wrapped in plastic and stored at room temperature for up to 1 day.)

6 *To make the ganache:* While the meringue layers cool, add the chocolate chips to a medium heat-safe bowl. Heat the cream in a small saucepan until it comes to a simmer, then pour it over the chocolate. Cover the top of the bowl with plastic wrap and set aside for 5 minutes, then remove the plastic wrap and whisk to combine. The ganache should be smooth and glossy.

(Optional: Spread ¼ cup of ganache into a thin yet opaque layer onto a piece of waxed or parchment paper and place on a plate in the refrigerator to chill for making shaved chocolate to decorate the top of the cake.)

7 *To make the whipped cream:* Add the cream, granulated sugar, and vanilla to the bowl of a stand mixer fitted with the whisk attachment. Whip on high speed until the cream forms medium-stiff peaks, 1½ to 2 minutes. Turn off the mixer and add the powdered sugar, then whip on medium speed just to combine, about 10 seconds.

8 Carefully remove one meringue disk from the parchment and place on a plate. Use an offset spatula to cover it with all of the ganache, then spread with about ¾ cup of whipped cream. Place another meringue disk on top and spread with the fruit preserves and then ¾ cup of whipped cream. Set the third meringue disk on top and spread the remaining whipped cream over the top and sides of the cake.

9 Decorate with the tiny meringues. (If making chocolate curls, use a chef's knife to shave the chilled ganache from the parchment paper and sprinkle it over the top.) Chill the cake for at least 30 minutes before serving. The cake is best served cold from the refrigerator and should be eaten within 1 day of assembling. Slice with a serrated knife and serve.

GLUTEN–FREE BÛCHE DE NOËL *Makes 1 log serving 8 to 10*

Meringue Mushrooms
2 large egg whites

½ teaspoon cream of tartar

¼ cup granulated sugar

½ cup powdered sugar

Unsweetened cocoa powder, for dusting

Chocolate Roulade
1 tablespoon unsalted butter, for greasing the pan

9 tablespoons Dutch-processed cocoa powder

9 large eggs, at room temperature

½ cup light brown sugar

½ teaspoon fine sea salt

Heaping ¾ cup finely chopped semisweet chocolate (about 4 ounces), melted

½ cup granulated sugar

Caffeinated Chocolate Mousse (page 186)

Chocolate Ganache Frosting
2⅓ cups finely chopped semisweet chocolate (about 12 ounces)

¾ cup heavy cream

Matcha powder, for decorating the cake

Indulgent, airy, *and* gluten-free, this ganache-frosted chocolate mousse–filled yule log is decadent but not too rich, and, since there isn't any flour or butter in it, it stays light and airy. The true magic in making a bûche de Noël (often called a Yule log) is in the accessorizing—I love to make white mushrooms out of meringue. It's also fun to play with chocolate shavings or gold dust to make them resemble tree bark. Along with the gingerbread castle on page 254, this is a great recipe to really expand the depths of your creative self. Now break out those dragées and get sprinkling! The cake is also excellent filled with the chestnut cream on page 247.

1 *To make the meringue mushrooms:* Preheat the oven to 375°F and line a rimmed sheet pan with parchment paper. Add the egg whites to the bowl of a stand mixer fitted with the whisk attachment. Whip the whites on medium-high speed until they become foamy, about 20 seconds. Add the cream of tartar and gradually sprinkle in the granulated sugar, continuing to whip the whites until they hold soft peaks, 30 seconds to 1 minute longer. Use a sieve to add the powdered sugar to the whites and continue to beat until the whites hold stiff peaks, about 30 seconds longer.

2 Fit a pastry bag with a round tip and add some meringue to the bag. Pipe the meringue onto the parchment-lined pan, creating five ½"- to 1"-long mushroom stems (ranging in length, just as some mushrooms are short and some are tall) and five caps, some the size of a quarter, some a little larger. Continue to make meringue caps and stems until you run out of meringue. Bake the meringue until it is dry to the touch, about 1½ hours. Remove from the oven and cool completely.

3 *To make the chocolate roulade:* Grease a rimmed half sheet pan (18" x 13") with the butter. Line the pan with a sheet of parchment paper, pressing it down to stick to the butter, then turn the parchment over so the greased side faces up. Sift 1 tablespoon of cocoa over the parchment and tap the pan to evenly disperse it.

recipe continues

4 Crack the eggs, separating the whites into a bowl and the yolks into the bowl of a stand mixer fitted with the whisk attachment. Set the whites aside. Beat the yolks on medium-high speed until pale and creamy, about 2 minutes. Add the brown sugar and salt and continue to beat until thick, about 2 minutes longer. Reduce the speed to low and add the melted chocolate; once the chocolate is combined, turn off the mixer, remove the bowl, and sift in 6 tablespoons of the cocoa. Use a whisk to fold the cocoa into the egg yolk mixture and then transfer it to a large bowl.

5 Clean the bowl and whisk attachment well, then add the egg whites to the bowl. Whisk the whites on medium-high speed until they are foamy, about 30 seconds. While whisking, sprinkle in the granulated sugar slowly and steadily, continuing to whip until the whites hold stiff peaks, about 3 minutes. Whisk half of the whites into the chocolate mixture to lighten it, then fold in the remaining whites.

6 Transfer the cake batter to the prepared sheet pan, using a rubber spatula to even out the batter and smooth the top as best as possible. Bake the cake until it pulls away from the sides and the center resists light pressure, about 20 minutes, rotating the pan midway through baking. Remove the cake from the oven and use a paring knife to separate the sides from the pan.

7 Add the remaining 2 tablespoons of cocoa to a sieve and sift the cocoa over the hot cake. Immediately lay a clean kitchen towel over the cake (one that won't leave lint behind), then invert it onto a cutting board. Peel off and discard the parchment. Roll the cake up, starting with the short side (yes, you are rolling the cake and towel together!). Set aside to cool for 30 minutes.

8 Unroll the cake and remove the towel. Use an offset spatula to spread the mousse over the cake, evening it out as best as possible, then roll the cake up again. Turn it seam side down on a cake platter or foil-lined sheet pan. Wrap the pan in plastic wrap and refrigerate while you make the ganache frosting.

9 *To make the chocolate ganache frosting:* Add the chocolate to a medium heat-safe bowl. Bring the cream to a near boil in a small saucepan over high heat, then pour the cream over the chocolate. Cover the bowl with plastic wrap and set aside for 5 minutes, then remove the plastic wrap and whisk until the mixture is smooth and glossy. Take about ½ cup of the ganache and spread it thinly and evenly over a baking mat or piece of parchment paper. Set it aside or refrigerate (this will become your chocolate for making curls to decorate the log). Depending on the warmth of your room, the ganache will take 10 to 30 minutes to cool and thicken to an easily spreadable consistency.

10 Remove the roulade from the refrigerator and discard the plastic wrap. Place it on the platter you will use for serving. Use an offset spatula to frost the top and sides of the roulade, using long strokes to create deep indentions that will make it look like the bark of a tree. Refrigerate the roulade to firm the frosting. Meanwhile, peel up the chocolate you set aside on the baking mat, using a butter knife to peel it up into curls for decorating the log (if the chocolate was refrigerated, let it sit at room temperature for about 10 minutes before making curls so the chocolate doesn't snap or crack).

11 Dust the mushrooms with some cocoa. Use the tip of a paring knife to make a small hole in the middle of each meringue mushroom cap and fit a stem in (trim the stem into a point if needed to get it to fit). Add the matcha powder to a sieve and tap it over the log to make it look mossy. Stick the mushrooms on and around the log. Add the chocolate curls to the log and serve.

Bûche Ahead

True, there are many moving parts to making a bûche de Noël. Make the components over a few days and then really enjoy yourself when it comes time to assemble and decorate the cake.

Meringue Mushrooms: You can make the mushrooms up to 3 days ahead of time (if it's humid, the meringues may not stay crisp, though they will hold up); keep them in an airtight container and assemble when you decorate the cake.

Chocolate Mousse: Make the mousse first. It holds in the fridge for up to 3 days.

Chocolate Roulade and Chocolate Ganache Frosting: Make the cake and the ganache on the same day that you plan to fill and roll the cake. The filled, rolled cake keeps unfrosted in the fridge for 1 day (wrap the platter well in plastic wrap)—after that, it will dry out. Once frosted, it will keep a few days as well (the ganache seals in the moisture). Let it sit out at room temperature for 20 minutes before slicing and serving.

PEAR-FRANGIPANE TART *Makes one 9¹/₂" tart*

½ recipe chilled My Favorite Pie Dough (page 50)

3 tablespoons unsalted butter

2 large eggs

½ cup granulated sugar

1 tablespoon vanilla extract

1 teaspoon fine sea salt

¼ teaspoon almond extract

1½ cups almond flour or meal

7 poached pear halves (from 3½ pears, page 180)

This classic French tart is simply one of my favorite desserts. It is elegant and delicate, perfumed by the mix of honey-poached pears and the aroma of sweet almond frangipane, a nutty, airy cream filling that serves as the cushion for the pears. The recipe also works well with poached apples and travels beautifully if you want to bring it to a party or dinner as a holiday gift (it is delicious for up to 5 days after baking). I serve it with a dollop of whipped cream that is sweetened with just a touch of sugar and a pinch of lemon zest.

1   Set a long piece of parchment paper or plastic wrap on your work surface and place the pie dough on top. Cover with another sheet of parchment or plastic wrap and roll into a 10" circle. Peel away the top layer of parchment or plastic and invert the dough into a 9½" tart pan, carefully fitting it into the sides and ridges of the pan. Use a knife to trim off the overhang and refrigerate for 20 minutes. Preheat the oven to 375°F.

2   While the dough chills, brown the butter: Add the butter to a small saucepan or skillet over medium heat. Once the butter is melted, continue to cook it, tilting the pan to swirl the butter often, until it is mahogany and fragrant like toasted nuts, 3 to 4 minutes. Turn off the heat and pour the butter into a heat-safe cup (like a ramekin), leaving the browned bits behind in the pan. Set the butter aside to cool.

3   Line the tart pan with a sheet of parchment or aluminum foil, allowing the excess to drape over the edges. Add enough pie weights, dried beans, or rice to the pan to weigh down the paper. Bake the tart shell until the dough has lost its raw appearance and the edges are slightly golden, 17 to 20 minutes. Remove the pan from the oven and set aside to cool enough to remove the parchment and pie weights. Set the tart shell aside.

4 To make the frangipane, add the eggs, sugar, vanilla, salt, and almond extract to the bowl of a food processor and process until combined and creamy, about 15 seconds. Pulse in the cooled browned butter, then add the almond flour and process until smooth.

5 Use a rubber spatula to scrape the frangipane into the baked tart shell. Place a poached pear half on your work surface, cored side down, and use a paring knife to thinly slice it horizontally without slicing all the way through the pear—it should have an accordion effect. Repeat with the other pear halves. Place the pear halves in the tart with the narrow point facing the center, then place one in the very middle.

6 Set the tart on a baking sheet in the oven and bake until the pears have singed edges, the frangipane is golden brown and puffed, and the edges of the tart are browned, 30 to 40 minutes (reduce the oven temperature to 350°F if the tart edges are browning too quickly). Remove from the oven and cool completely before slicing.

GRAPPA–SUGAR PLUM
TART *Makes one 9" tart*

½ cup (1 stick) unsalted butter

1 tablespoon granulated sugar

½ teaspoon fine sea salt

1 cup all-purpose flour

2 large eggs

Juice of ½ lemon, plus 1 strip lemon zest

½ cup packed light brown sugar

6 pieces crystallized ginger, finely chopped

5 firm (but not hard) red- or purple-skinned plums, halved and pitted

¼ cup grappa

Ginger or vanilla ice cream or whipped cream, for serving

The real sugar plums in the poem "'Twas the Night before Christmas" aren't really plums at all but little knobs of seeds, nuts, and ground spices enrobed in a hard sugar glaze— and yes, they're about the size of a plum! I can't resist taking the poem a bit literally and buying some red plums at the market to make a sugar plum tart for the holiday table. The purple of the plum skins bleeds into the sugar syrup sauce, making the fruit a gorgeous and rich fuchsia color, while the crust poufs around the fruit almost like a Dutch pancake. Instead of pie dough or tart dough, I use cream puff pastry dough (called choux paste). It's very easy to make—just make the dough in a soup pot, chill it, and press into the pan, and that's it! You can also use store-bought puff pastry instead . . . I won't tell! (The sugar plum filling is also great canned on its own and given away as holiday gifts—it tastes so seasonally apropos even though it's technically out of season!)

1 To make the crust, add the butter to a medium saucepan over medium heat. Pour in 1 cup of water, then add the granulated sugar and salt. Whisk occasionally until the butter is completely melted. Turn off the heat and add the flour, using a wooden spoon to mix it until it comes together into a glossy ball that cleans the sides of the pan. Transfer the dough to a medium bowl and set aside to cool for 15 minutes, stirring occasionally to let steam escape.

2 Add the eggs to the dough one at a time, using a wooden spoon to stir between each addition. Set the dough onto a large piece of plastic wrap and use another piece of plastic wrap to press it into a circular and flat disk no more than ¾" to 1" thick. Refrigerate the dough until it is firm but not hard, about 1 hour (if refrigerating for longer, let the dough sit out at room temperature for 20 minutes to warm up before continuing).

3 Set a 9" springform cake pan on your work surface. Unclasp the sides and remove the bottom of the pan, then wrap it in aluminum foil. Insert it in the springform ring and clasp the pan to secure it. Unwrap the dough and place it in the bottom of the pan, pressing it out to the edges and about halfway up the sides—you want it to be about ¼" thick (you can use the bottom of a metal measuring cup to even the thickness of the bottom and sides if you like). Place the pan in the refrigerator overnight to chill the dough.

4 The next day, start the plums: Add 1 cup of water to a wide saucepan or medium pot. Stir in the lemon juice and the brown sugar, then sprinkle in the ginger and drop in the lemon zest. Place the plums cut side down in the pan so they all fit in an even layer. Bring the liquid to a simmer over medium-high heat and pour in the grappa. Reduce the heat to medium and gently simmer until the plums are tender and the liquid is reduced by half, about 20 minutes. Turn off the heat and set aside to cool to room temperature.

5 Adjust an oven rack to the lower-middle position and pre-heat the oven to 450°F. Wrap the bottom of the springform pan in foil so no plum juices leak out. Add the plums to the tart (save the poaching liquid for another use), cut side down, placing 1 plum in the middle. Bake for 15 minutes, then reduce the oven temperature to 375°F. Continue to bake the tart until the pastry is golden brown, puffed, and crisp, about 1½ hours.

6 Remove from the oven and cool for at least 1 hour before unclasping the pan and removing the tart. Slice and serve with ice cream or whipped cream.

CHOCOLATE CROISSANT BREAD PUDDING *Serves 6*

2 tablespoons unsalted butter

4–5 medium to large chocolate croissants, cut into bite-size pieces (about 6 cups)

3 cups heavy cream

2 large eggs, plus 2 large egg yolks

¾ cup granulated sugar

2 teaspoons vanilla extract

¼ teaspoon sea salt

Powdered sugar, for serving

Talk about excess! I came up with this idea when I had a few chocolate croissants left over after hosting a brunch. I had heard of plain croissants being turned into bread pudding, so why not chocolate croissants? I cut them up, gave them a quick toasting in the oven, then made a custard base with eggs and sugar. It's so rich and fantastic, and the smell wafting from your kitchen will transcend you to nirvana. It is also especially easy to make and holds beautifully for a morning brunch or an evening dessert (bake it off in individual ramekins or tiny cast-iron skillets so each guest can have his or her own).

1 Preheat the oven to 350°F. Grease a 1½-quart baking dish with the butter. Place the croissant pieces on a rimmed sheet pan and toast in the oven until golden brown, 5 to 7 minutes (the croissants will brown quickly since they have so much butter).

2 Meanwhile, whisk the cream, eggs, egg yolks, granulated sugar, vanilla, and salt together in a large bowl. Add the toasted croissant pieces and stir to soak them all, then transfer the croissant pieces and the liquid to the greased baking dish.

3 Bake until the croissant is set in the custard and everything is golden, 20 to 25 minutes.

4 Remove from the oven and cool for at least 15 minutes before serving sprinkled with powdered sugar. This is delicious warm, at room temperature, or cold.

CHESTNUT CREAM PUFFS *Makes 2 dozen*

Chestnut Cream

2 cups heavy cream

½ cup granulated sugar

2 teaspoons vanilla extract (or vanilla bean paste or 1 vanilla bean, split)

1½ cups packed chestnut purée (about 10 ounces; see note on page 249)

⅔ cup powdered sugar, sifted

Pâte à Choux

½ cup (1 stick) unsalted butter

2 teaspoons vanilla extract

1 tablespoon granulated sugar

¼ teaspoon fine sea salt

1 cup bread flour, sifted

4 large eggs plus 1 large egg white

Shortly after I launched my company in 2001, I found myself in Paris's legendary Belleville neighborhood with my sister, Alexandra, and some friends for dinner at a little hidden gem of a place. The six-table spot was a favorite of our hostess, Maria Luisa, the owner of the eponymous and legendary boutique on rue Cambon. The meal was pure traditional French country food, including terrines and pâtés that looked like beautifully marbled terrazzo, a deep and rich French onion soup (still the best I've *ever* eaten), and the most perfect crisp and airy pâte à choux cream puff shells. The wine flowed and the conversation switched from English to French and back again. Alexandra, who is fluent in French, translated for me as my tablemates (including the extraordinary Azzedine Alaïa) spoke in a rapid back-and-forth. It was a magical night, and every time I'm in Paris, I always try to find that restaurant, but it somehow eludes me. Luckily, I can now make pâte à choux to bring me right back into that moment from the comfort of my own New York City kitchen. I fill the shells with a chestnut whipped cream that is just sweet enough. It's a perfect ending to a winter holiday dinner.

1 *To start the chestnut cream:* Place ½ cup of the cream, the granulated sugar, and the vanilla in a medium saucepan and bring the cream to a gentle simmer over medium heat, stirring to dissolve the sugar. Reduce the heat to low and add the chestnut purée. Stir the purée and cream together as best as you can (the purée can be quite solid), cover the pan, and cook, stirring occasionally, until the purée softens, 3 to 4 minutes. Turn off the heat and let the mixture sit until cool, about 30 minutes. Transfer the mixture to a food processor or use an immersion blender to purée. Scrape the chestnut mixture into a medium bowl and set aside.

2 *To make the pâte à choux:* Preheat the oven to 400°F. Melt the butter in a medium saucepan over medium heat. Once the butter starts to bubble, reduce the heat to low. Add the vanilla, granulated sugar, and salt, stirring to dissolve. Turn off the

recipe continues

Buying Chestnuts

If you think I am roasting chestnuts at home, think again! I buy my chestnuts already peeled, cooked, and puréed—the purée is very thick, which is why I soften it in warm vanilla cream before stirring in sweetened whipped cream. Be sure to read the label on the can of chestnut purée so you know there isn't any added sugar or flavorings. If you can't find puréed chestnuts, you can use jars or bags of peeled and steamed chestnuts. In this case, you'll need about 2 cups of whole chestnuts (about 10 ounces). Chop them up and add them to the cream when you simmer it with the sugar and vanilla (instead of adding them at the end as you do if using chestnut purée), letting the chestnuts soften in the cream for 20 minutes before blending using an immersion blender or a food processor. (Or, if you have a high-powered blender, you can try blending the mixture with that, though it may be too stiff for standard home blenders.)

heat, add the flour, and stir vigorously to eliminate any lumps. Once the flour mixture collects into a dough ball and cleans the sides and bottom of the saucepan, transfer the mixture to the bowl of a stand mixer fitted with the whisk attachment. Turn the mixer on medium-low and add the whole eggs and egg white one at a time, whisking well between each addition.

3 Use a rubber spatula to transfer the mixture to a pastry bag fitted with a round tip (or to a resealable plastic bag, then slice off one corner to create a ½" to ¾" hole). Smear a little of the pâte à choux onto each corner of a rimmed sheet pan, then place a sheet of parchment paper on top and press it onto the corners (the pâte à choux helps the paper stay in place). Pipe the paste into about twenty-four 1½" rounds, leaving about 1" between each one. Use a wet finger to flatten out the top of each one.

4 Bake the pâte à choux for 10 minutes, then reduce the oven temperature to 350°F and continue to bake until the puffs are evenly golden and very dry, about 30 minutes longer. Remove from the oven and set aside to cool. (The shells can be baked up to 1 day before filling—store them in an airtight container and recrisp in a 350°F oven for 5 to 10 minutes if necessary before cooling and filling as described in step 6.)

5 *To finish the chestnut cream:* Pour the remaining 1½ cups of cream into the bowl of a stand mixer fitted with the whisk attachment. Add the powdered sugar and beat the mixture on medium-low speed to combine. Increase the mixer speed to medium-high and beat until the cream forms medium-stiff peaks. Add half of the cream to the chestnut mixture and whisk to combine. Add the remaining cream mixture and whisk until smooth. (The chestnut cream can be made and refrigerated in an airtight container up to 1 day before using.)

6 Slice the cream puff shells in half so they have a top and a bottom—the center should be hollow. Spoon about 2 tablespoons into the bottom half and gently set the top half in place. Place on a platter and repeat with the remaining shells. The cream puffs are best filled right before serving; or, fill and refrigerate for up to 1 hour before serving. The filled cream puffs will soften the longer they sit in the fridge, but they still taste great!

CROQUEMBOUCHE

Cardboard cake circle or a large flat circular platter on which to build the croquembouche

Poster board

Heavy-duty clear tape

A double batch of cream puff shells (page 247)

2 cups granulated sugar

Making a croquembouche takes a bit of work and dedication, but the payoff is so worth it. You can create a gorgeous pyramid of pastry all surrounded by a thin and intricate web of caramel-colored spun sugar . . . and the best thing is that it is totally edible! Break off a knob and crunch down for a deliciously sweet and cookie-like confection. Most people fill the cream puff shells with pastry cream, but I leave mine empty for a few reasons: (a) it cuts down on the prep time; (b) the croquembouche is lighter in weight and easier to build and carry; (c) it takes away some of the guilt of going in for seconds, thirds, and fourths; (d) you can leave the tower out at room temperature for a longer time without worrying about the shells getting soggy. Creating this centerpiece dessert reminds me of making a gown, and the reaction is similar—just pure "wow."

1 Make the cone on which to build the croquembouche: If using a cardboard cake circle, cover it with foil or pretty paper so you don't see the cardboard. Cut your poster board into a half circle. The bigger the half circle, the bigger the cone and the more pastry shells you'll need to surround it and cover it up. I find that for 48 (a double batch) of cream puff shells, a 14" half circle works out well. Make a small notch in the center of the straight side of the half circle base—this will be your point at the tip-top of the cone. Now twist the half circle into a cone shape and tape it from the inside to hold it together. Place the cone on the circle—there should be at least a 3" border around the edge of the bottom of the cone and the edge of the base.

2 Add the sugar to a medium saucepan over medium heat. Melt the sugar until it liquefies and starts to bubble on the top, swirling the pan occasionally to encourage even melting. Reduce the heat to medium-low and continue to cook, swirling the contents of the pan occasionally, until the sugar is caramel colored—not dark mahogany but more of a deep butterscotch. Remove it from the heat. Now you have to work quickly!

recipe continues

3 Use tongs to dip the bottom of a cream puff shell in the hot caramel and then stick it on top of the base at the edge of the cone. Continue with the next cream puff shell until you have made a ring around the base of the cone. Now continue with the next layer, setting a caramel-dipped cream puff shell on top of the first layer so it is like stacking bricks, with the second layer resting not directly on top of the first but directly on top of two cream puff shells beneath it. Continue to make the second layer, then the third, fourth, and so forth. Place the final cream puff shell on top to make a point, like a Christmas tree. If at any point the caramel becomes too hard to dip, set it over heat to liquefy it.

4 Now it's time to make the spun sugar (some call this caramel floss). Set a large metal bowl upside down. Dip a fork into the caramel (put the saucepan over medium heat to re-liquefy it if needed) and, using a quick back-and-forth motion with your arm, make strings over the bowl. They will be very thin and delicate! Once you have a thick mass, pick up the strands and drape them around the croquembouche. Continue until you have enough sugar to wrap around the entire croquembouche. Set onto your table and prepare to stun your guests!

PAIN D'ÉPICES *Makes one 9" loaf*

5 tablespoons unsalted
butter, at room
temperature

3½ cups all-purpose
flour, plus extra for
flouring the pan

½ cup dark rye flour

2½ teaspoons baking
soda

1½ teaspoons ground
cinnamon

1½ teaspoons ground
ginger

¼ teaspoon freshly
grated nutmeg

¼ teaspoon ground
cloves

½ teaspoon salt

½ teaspoon whole
anise seeds

¼ teaspoon freshly
ground black pepper

1 large egg

1 cup honey

1 tablespoon finely
grated orange zest
(from about 2 oranges)

Pain d'épices is a French version of an unsweetened spice cake. It makes the most wonderful afternoon snack when you're foraging around for something that barely hints of sweet. You can toast it or dress it up with a bit of sweet butter or jam for a richer flavor, or use slices of pain d'épices to make an impromptu strawberry shortcake, piling on the berries and cream between a few moist slices. I was inspired by Martine Niquet in Paris to make a pain d'épices and adapted this recipe from a classic book by master baker Flo Braker, *Baking for All Occasions*, one of my favorite baking books. It has now become an annual holiday tradition.

1 Preheat the oven to 350°F. Use 1 tablespoon of the butter to grease the sides and bottom of a 9" loaf pan, then add 2 table-spoons of flour, shaking it around to evenly coat the bottom and sides. Tap out any excess and set the pan aside.

2 Sift together the all-purpose flour, rye flour, baking soda, cinnamon, ginger, nutmeg, cloves, and salt into a bowl. Stir in the anise seeds and pepper.

3 Add the remaining 4 tablespoons of butter to the bowl of a stand mixer fitted with the paddle attachment (or a large bowl if using a hand mixer). Beat on medium speed until light and creamy. Reduce the speed to medium-low and add the egg, honey, and orange zest. With the mixer running, add 1 cup of water, then add the dry ingredients in three additions, scraping the sides and bottom of the bowl as needed. Once all of the flour is added, increase the speed to medium and mix until smooth and well combined, about 30 seconds.

4 Use a rubber spatula to transfer the batter to the prepared loaf pan, smoothing out the top. Bake until the top is somewhat dark (totally normal), the center of the cake resists light pressure, and a cake tester inserted into the center comes out clean, about 1 hour.

5 Cool the cake for 10 minutes, then tip the cake out of the loaf pan and onto a wire rack. Cool completely before slicing and serving. Wrapped well in plastic wrap, the cake will keep for up to 1 week stored at room temperature.

CHRISTMAS MORNING
GINGERBREAD CASTLE

My favorite memories of Christmas morning are not of opening gifts, but spending time planning elaborate gingerbread structures with my mom. New York City always has a special kind of quiet on holidays because so many people head out of town. My mom and I would bake flat slabs of gingerbread in shapes that would form the walls and roofs of houses and castles. After they were baked and cooled, we would glue them together with royal icing—and then the real fun began! We'd melt sugar to make the "glass" for windows, line the walkways to our gingerbread structures with mint swirls or bits of red licorice, and stick pastel-colored Necco wafers to tile the roof. There was no limit, and believe me, I went to town. The gingerbread structures would stay poised in a place of honor in our Spring Street loft for months with only a few nibbles going missing over time! I still enjoy making a beautiful gingerbread house (or castle).

GINGERBREAD COOKIES

Makes 2 to 3 dozen cookies (depending on the size of your cookie cutters)

Gingerbread

3 cups all-purpose flour

2 teaspoons ground cinnamon

2 teaspoons ground ginger

1 teaspoon baking soda

½ teaspoon ground allspice

½ teaspoon ground cloves

½ teaspoon fine sea salt

¾ cup (1½ sticks) unsalted butter, at room temperature

½ cup packed dark brown sugar

¼ cup granulated sugar

1 large egg

¼ cup molasses

1 teaspoon vanilla extract

Icing

2 cups powdered sugar

5–7 tablespoons heavy cream

A few drops of food coloring (optional)

Sprinkles, decorative pearls, mini chocolate chips, licorice ropes (optional)

Every year at holiday time, we throw a party for the company. If I don't bring homemade gingerbread cookies, there is an office-wide revolt! I like to bring platters of undecorated cookies and a few piping bags filled with colored icing so everyone can have fun decorating the cookies with their own ideas for dresses and ties and accessorize them with edible silver pearls, sprinkles, and chocolate chips!

1   *To make the gingerbread:* Whisk the flour, cinnamon, ginger, baking soda, allspice, cloves, and salt together in a large bowl.

2   Add the butter to the bowl of a stand mixer fitted with the paddle attachment (or to a large bowl if using a hand mixer) and cream on medium speed until light and creamy, about 1 minute. Add the brown sugar and granulated sugar and cream on medium-high speed until pale and airy, about 2 minutes. Reduce the mixer speed to medium-low and add the egg, mixing until well combined. Use a rubber spatula to scrape down the sides of the bowl.

3   Add the molasses and vanilla to the butter mixture and beat on medium speed until no streaks remain. Reduce the speed to low and add the flour mixture. Mix until most of the flour is incorporated, then increase the speed to medium-low and cream until the dough comes together and no more white streaks remain, 20 to 30 seconds.

4   Place half of the dough on a sheet of parchment paper, cover with another sheet of parchment, and use a rolling pin to roll it into a ¼"-thick sheet. Slide the sheet of dough onto a baking sheet. Repeat with the other half of the dough. Refrigerate the dough until it is firm, at least 30 minutes or up to overnight (if refrigerating for overnight or longer, make sure the dough is

recipe continues

well covered with plastic wrap or that the parchment is well tucked so the dough doesn't dry out).

5 Adjust one oven rack to the upper-middle position and another to the lower-middle position and preheat the oven to 350°F. Remove a baking sheet from the refrigerator and slide one sheet of dough onto your work surface. Remove the top sheet of parchment and use it to line a rimmed sheet pan. Use cookie cutters to stamp shapes out from the dough, then slide a knife or mini offset spatula under the shapes and transfer the cut-out gingerbread to the prepared sheet pan. Gather the scraps and set aside (don't press them together yet). Repeat with the other sheet of dough and a second sheet pan. Gather all of the scraps and gently press them together. (Don't knead them into a perfect ball or you will overwork the dough and have tough cookies! The dough will even out when you roll it.) Roll out the dough until it is ¼" thick and cut out as many cookies as you can. Divide them among the sheet pans (or transfer them to a plate and save them for a third round of baking). Discard any remaining scraps.

6 Bake the cookies until they are golden brown and a little darker around the edges, 8 to 10 minutes. Remove from the oven and cool for 5 minutes before transferring them to a wire rack to cool completely. (The cookies must be completely cooled before icing.)

7 *To make the icing:* While the cookies cool, whisk the powdered sugar and 5 tablespoons of the cream together in a medium bowl until completely smooth. If the icing seems too thick, add more cream a little at a time until you get your desired consistency (the more you add, the thinner and more glaze-like and less opaque your icing will be). You can divide the icing among a few smaller bowls and add a drop of food coloring to make different colors (I always keep some pure white). Fit icing bags with fine tips and add the icing to them. Decorate the cookies as you like, using the icing and sprinkles, decorative pearls, chocolate chips, or licorice ropes, if desired.

FLOURLESS CHOCOLATE CAKE

Makes one 9" cake

¾ cup (1½ sticks) chilled unsalted butter, plus 1 tablespoon at room temperature

12 ounces 60% cacao semi- or bittersweet chocolate, finely chopped

6 large eggs

½ cup Frangelico hazelnut liqueur

1 cup lightly packed light brown sugar

¼ teaspoon fine sea salt

6 ounces blanched, untoasted hazelnuts, finely ground (about 1½ cups)

Powdered sugar, for serving

This is a smashing cake, and the fact that it doesn't contain any flour, but instead relies on finely ground hazelnuts, is nothing short of amazing. Don't expect it to rise as high as a cake with flour would—it is really more like an extra-dense, chocolatey, and moist torte. Its richness seems to intensify the next day (if it hasn't been consumed by then!). It is lovely baked as a large single-layer cake but can also be made in ramekins to serve as individual personalized cakes.

1   Preheat the oven to 350°F. Lightly coat a 9" springform pan with the 1 tablespoon of room temperature butter. Set the pan on a sheet of parchment paper and trace a circle around the outside of the pan. Cut out the circle and place it in the pan bottom, pressing down to fit it into the pan. Turn the paper over and press down again (now both sides are greased for easy removal after baking!). Wrap the bottom of the springform pan in aluminum foil, making sure the foil comes at least 1" up the pan sides.

2   Cut the remaining ¾ cup of butter into a few pieces and add them to a medium heat-safe bowl with the chocolate. Add 1" of water to a medium saucepan and bring the water to a boil over high heat. Reduce the heat to low and set the bowl with the butter and chocolate over the water (make sure the bottom of the bowl doesn't sit in the water). Melt the butter and the chocolate together, stirring often, until completely smooth, about 5 minutes. Remove the bowl from the saucepan and set aside (the chocolate and butter mixture should be completely melted but not hot).

3   Whisk the eggs in a large bowl until they are foamy, then add the Frangelico, brown sugar, and salt, whisking until the

recipe continues

sugar is completely dissolved. Whisk a little of the egg mixture into the chocolate mixture. Continue to add the egg mixture a little at a time until the chocolate mixture is cool to the touch, then use a rubber spatula to scrape all of the chocolate mixture into the remaining egg mixture, whisking well to combine. Gently fold in the hazelnuts and use a rubber spatula to transfer the cake batter to the prepared springform pan.

4 Set the springform pan in a roasting pan or on a rimmed sheet pan and place it on the middle oven rack. Add enough water to the pan to reach ½" up the sides of the pan, then bake the cake until a cake tester inserted into the center comes out with just a crumb or two attached, about 1½ hours. Cool completely before running a knife around the edges of the pan to release the cake from the pan sides. Unclasp the sides of the pan and invert the cake onto a cake plate. Remove the parchment circle and dust the top with powdered sugar, then slice and serve.

DOUBLE DECKER APRICOT VARIATION
Once the cake is fully baked and cooled, invert it from the pan onto a cake plate. Use a serrated knife to mark the sides of the cake in four spots. Begin to slice through the cake, turning it a little as you slice and using the marks as your guide. Steer the knife through the center of the cake so you have two even halves. Carefully slide a spatula beneath the top layer and slide it onto a cake round or large rimless plate (so it lies flat). Spread about ¾ cup of apricot jam on top of the bottom layer. Place the top cake layer over the jam and dust with powdered sugar or glaze with the ganache on page 182.

ACKNOWLEDGMENTS

I wish to thank those who have been so generous contributing their creativity and inspiration to *Cooking with Zac*—I am filled with gratitude: Susan Posen, Stephen Posen, Christopher Niquet, Raquel Pelzel, Victoria Granof, Pamela Duncan Silver, Anna Williams, Ava Imperio, Jacqueline Schnabel, Stella Schnabel, Lola Schnabel, Margherita Missoni, Nancy Westheimer, Karen Orzack-Moore, David Kuhn, Marisa Vigilante, Reika Yo, Elisabeth Holder Raberin, Katie Holmes, Kevin Sharkey, Martha Stewart, Zezé and Peggy at Zezé Flowers, Joan Nathan, Jason Weinberg, James Adams, and last but not least Ron Burkle. Bon appétit!

INDEX

Underscored page references indicate sidebars. **Boldface** references indicate photographs.